Landscape Change in the Scottish Highlands

Imagination and Reality

James Fenton

"This living flowing land is all there is, forever"
Gary Snyder, from 'By Frazier Creek Falls'

Whittles Publishing

Whittles Publishing Ltd.,
Dunbeath,
Caithness, KW6 6EG,
Scotland, UK

www.whittlespublishing.com

Printed and bound by CPI Group (UK) Ltd, Croydon, CR0 4YY

Cover: A romantic view of the traditional Highland landscape c. 1900 by the Scottish landscape painter Douglas Cameron.

Contents

Preface

The Scottish Highlands strongly appeal to the public imagination and due to the writings of Sir Walter Scott they are now symbolic of Scotland as a whole: they are a land of mountains, glens and lochs, of golden eagles and red deer; a land with a rich cultural history of clans and clanship, of wars and resistance to authority, of kilts and castles, of crofts and crofting, of Highland cows and sheep, of music and dance. A land still wild and where the trappings of modern civilisation can be shaken off.

But how does this imagined landscape relate to the actuality on the ground? Is it a wild landscape that has escaped the pressures of the modern world, or is such untrammelled wildness only in the mind?

The aim of this book is to answer this last question by taking an objective look at the history of the Highland landscape, how it has changed over the centuries and how it is still changing. It should be pointed out that the word 'landscape' itself is rather a vague term, meaning different things to different people. A 'landscape' is what we perceive when we look around us: a combination of physical landform, of the vegetation covering it, of associated human structures ancient and modern, coloured by the understandings each of us holds within ourselves (which may or may not accord with reality). Those with a knowledge of ecology will perceive the same landscape differently to those with a knowledge of cultural history. Hence, the book opens with a demonstration of how the Highland landscape can be perceived differently by different people.

Toman Còinnich & Sgùrr Breac, Fannich Hills, Wester Ross.

There are many books on the history of the physical landscape, on the underlying geology and the processes such as glaciation and erosion that have created the landforms we have today. This book does not cover this aspect but, because the vegetation cloaking the land is such an important part of the landscape, it focuses instead on how the overlay of vegetation has changed over time.

Nowadays, much of the upland landscape is being transformed in the name of 'ecological restoration', but for restoration to be necessary there has to be evidence of past damage. The book offers a critique of the whole concept of ecological restoration when applied to the Highlands, in particular whether the landscape needs restoring in the first place. It is fashionable to talk about a 'biodiversity crisis', and although there is such a crisis over much of the planet, it is debatable as to whether such a crisis exists in the Highlands: if there is, it is being brought about by much of the action taking place under the restoration banner.

The book also explains the ways in which humans have impacted the landscape, and are continuing to do so, through management and the imposition of infrastructure. It compares the imagined landscape with the reality, discussing whether all these changes matter, and outlines what needs to be done if we think it important to conserve at least some locations where the imagined wild Highland landscape still exists.

I hope this book will help people see the landscape of the Scottish Highlands through objective eyes and see it for what it is, rather than what we think it is. I also hope that the book will enable readers to identify the changes we are imposing on the land and, rather than just accepting all these changes as a fait accompli, debate the direction in which we want the landscape to go. There is a danger that the traditional Highland landscape of open hill will become so rare that we will only begin lamenting its loss when it is too late.

James Fenton
Isle of Seil

From Ben Alligin, Torridon, looking over Beinn Dearg towards Beinn Eighe.

Chapter 1 Introduction

Which landscape?

A degraded landscape

It is said that in the far-flung reaches of western Europe there exists a landscape of open hills and moors, of rivers and lochs, of islands and rocky coasts, a land long-occupied by people, but people who have been cavalier, overriding nature and imposing their will on the land. For there was once a great forest, the Forest of Caledon as named by the Romans, a rich forest that clothed the country from coast to coast and mountain top to sea, a natural forest, a home for many: the deer, the brown bear, the wolf and the lynx, and many lesser beasts.

But as soon as the shores were colonised by people, destruction began: at first the axe and fire to create space for settlement, and later the beasts brought in to make living possible – for meat, for milk, for clothing, for leather, for dung, and even for warmth – kept the trees at bay. Over the millennia, the forest was eaten away at the edges, the wildlife retreated and the trees only survived in distant corners. But these remaining woods were themselves doomed, for new landowners came and destroyed the remnants to feed the greed of the iron smelters; they introduced the sheep that grazed the land to the bone, allowing no forest to be reborn, and later they removed these "woolly maggots",[1] replacing them with red deer for the shooting, again allowing numbers to rise way above any natural balance, damaging both woods and peatland. In the east, they burnt the moors to smithereens for their red grouse to thrive.

The result is the degraded landscape inherited today, a wet desert and a devastated countryside, or, to put it scientifically and quoting the famous ecologist Frank Fraser Darling:[2]

> The Highlands, as a geologic and physiographic region, are unable to withstand deforestation and maintain productiveness and fertility. Their history has been one of steadily accelerating deforestation until the great mass of forests was gone, and thereafter of forms of land usage which prevented regeneration of tree growth and reduced the land to crude values and expressions of its solid geological composition. In short, the Highlands are a devastated countryside.

Indeed, 'everyone knows this', as the historian James Hunter implies:[3]

> If you want to understand the Highlands – instead of simply looking at them – you have to start by accepting that very little hereabouts is as nature intended ... Conservation organisations nowadays take for granted that the Highlands are degraded ecologically."

1

And more recently we are informed by Andrew Painting in his book *Regeneration*:[4]

> For many, Highland sporting culture, the deer, the grouse moors is what makes the Highlands special and beautiful. But for many others, the grazed, burned, drained moors and dying woodlands are a landscape of environmental and cultural destruction.

There is almost a moral imperative to restore this once-great landscape, to re-clothe the hills with trees and shrubs right to the very top, to let the rivers and lochs once more be lined with their missing trees, to bring back the full panoply of God's creation, to recreate a lost paradise. The few remaining fragments of the Caledonian Forest need to expand to their former glory. Stop! Rewrite!

A political landscape

Beyond the populous and fertile lowlands, northwards to the islands almost at the edge of the Arctic Circle, there is a great tract of empty land, land dispossessed of people, a barren land which should be rich with the sound of children's voices, of voices foreign to the south, land rich with music and dance – and with wildlife.

For centuries this land resisted the effete civilisation of the south, the energy of the people concentrated on mere survival in the unforgiving landscape, on inter-tribal wars, and on wars in defence of freedom from invasion: wars celebrated by the seannachie (the Gaelic storytellers), the feats of the great warriors passed down from generation to generation through poem and song. Warlike, yes, but also strong on family. The chief was father to the clan and they were supportive of each other – but always fiercely independent. To the southerner, the people of the land speaking an alien language were primitive and uncouth and unwilling to bow to regal authority; their land was dangerous to enter.

But this could not last in a world becoming more uniform and organised, and so, perhaps with inevitability, the land was tamed, the people conquered, the south gained full control and the land's fierce independence was lost, never to be regained. Over time the people were betrayed by their chiefs, chiefs unable to resist the luxuries the modern world was now providing, although a few resisted the temptations for many years. But the modern world was not cheap in monetary terms, and the old clan chiefs and their descendants exploited the clan's holdings to support their enjoyment of the effete civilisation they had once despised.

They disregarded their people, cleared them off their own land and created empty glens because the land was poor and richer pickings were to be had without a population to support. They disregarded the land, too, working no longer in harmony with nature as their forefathers had done, but destroying its very essence. They tore down the remaining trees for financial gain and to fuel the iron furnaces; they covered the land with sheep, which browsed away any remaining forest, and soon the sheep were replaced by too many deer so that the rich elite could have the land to themselves for the killing of animals, including any wild animal brave enough to defy them.

This rich elite, by their actions, destroyed the landscape, removing the final vestiges of natural woodland and converting former woods into barren grouse moor. But recent times have brought new hope. The people can take back the land, and have done so in many places. The children can grow young trees and shrubs for energetic groups to plant, to recreate the Great Forest of Caledon and the long-lost scrub that once clothed mountains to the highest tops. People from far and wide have sent money to help restore the land, and the government has plans to stop the extensive overgrazing by deer, their high numbers possible because there is no longer the wolf to eat them. These are deer that eat trees and trample the land to death – damaging peatlands in the process – helping to destroy both the land and the climate. Ministers also have plans to stop the burning of grouse moors so that, who knows, the forest might return even here.

There is also hope that the landowner has lost his sway, that this empty land can once again be full of people and children's voices, people, who instead of damaging nature will recreate the earthly paradise that their antecedents destroyed. Stop! Rewrite!

An economic landscape

If one ventures to the far periphery of Europe, to an area where the land itself ventures far into the ocean, there may be found a landscape where energy reigns supreme, where one Atlantic storm chases the heels of another, where the heat of the sun on these grey northern climes has been converted to ceaseless wind and ever-pouring rain – energy for the taking to feed our insatiable demand. And be taken it must, for what other use has the land than to provide for our needs, satisfy our wants and fund our ever-more extravagant lifestyles? And to save us from ourselves, because we need its energy to stave off the apocalypse of a planet too hot for our survival.

Blow, blow thou winter wind, thou summer wind, thou autumn wind. Let the turbines fly, let us squeeze every last kilowatt from the natural flows, let every hill and moor do its duty to its country. And of course there is energy to be had from the burns and rivers flowing wastefully down to the sea; every loch must be dammed, every watercourse piped. To quote Ian MacArthur, MP for Perth and East Perthshire from 1959 to 1974:[5]

> [I] saw this great dam rising out of the glen [and was] astonished not by the harm it had done to the beauty of the glen but by the way it had somehow improved the aspect before my eyes … a symbol of strength … new life … new hope.

But there is more to the hills than this: theirs is a land fit for trees – no matter where they originate – trees that store the energy of the sun, provide jobs and suit industry. Indeed, these trees are essential for the country to survive.

The sea, also, is a harvest of plenty, the wind, waves and tides if controlled for our use are an energy factory par excellence. So why not use it – the land and sea empty and wasteful no longer? Stop! Rewrite!

A wild, natural landscape

There is a wild landscape in the far northwest corner of Europe, whose shore is beaten by the eternal storms of the mighty Atlantic Ocean. It is a landscape of hills, lochs and glens, of unspoilt coasts and islands; nature still has the upper hand.

Here, mountains are not big and overbearing but open and clear-edged – when they can be seen through the all-embracing mist and cloud. On a rare gentle day, glowing with that special quality found in unpolluted air, a golden eagle soars above or an antlered stag is outlined against a clear horizon. In a snow-blasted blizzard on a short winter's day, the thought of coming home to a heart-warming peat fire fills the mind. This land is of wide-open, windswept moors where there is room to breathe and space to live. It offers no shelter and the wind gives no quarter; it is home only to the hardy – the red grouse and the blue hare. Long, snake-like lochs infiltrate the landscape and blur the distinction between land and sea; there is seaweed far from the sea. Here the sunsets are glorious but often they are backed by the gold-rimmed grey cloud-wracks that herald yet another storm.

This is a landscape where the elemental forces of nature are still in command, one where no human hand has determined the pattern of its vegetated cloak (where else in the world is this still true?). It is land mostly "in a state of nature", as the botanist James Robertson wrote in 1771,[6] although nowadays some would call it wild land, which survived because, as Haldane tells us,[7] it was largely unused and uncared for during the era of the clans. It is land that scientists say is internationally important.[8]

People have always lived here, at least since the retreat of the ice, but they have been confined to the few places where the soil is sufficiently fertile or where there is easy access to the sea, though there is always the backdrop of undeveloped hill. The people, Hunter states,[9] have a keen affinity with the land, which has inspired poets and travellers, ancient and modern. Rennie McOwan in his poem *The Things of the North* says:[10]

> Let us give thanks for the things of the north …
> For winds and rain that scour endless miles of rippling heather,
> for an elemental wildness that knows little of cities and towns,
> for an understanding that in stark harshness blinding beauty there abound
> for those who walk and seek to find …

It is a land that Lord Cockburn, who had a keen eye for landscape, extolled in 1853:[11]

> A brilliant, though cold day. But a glorious district …. O these large, heathery, silent hills.
> Treeless, peakless, and nearly rockless! Great masses of solitary silence, broken only by high

rills, tumbling into raging and sparkling torrents in the valley! And the gradual opening of the rich low country, ending in the beauty of Perth! Were I to see it yearly for a thousand years, I cannot conceive that the impression would ever fade.

Can these be the rantings of dishevelled minds? Does such a wild, natural landscape exist? Did it ever exist, or is it merely a landscape of the imagination?

* * *

Landscapes of the imagination. Surely the four outlined above – the degraded, the political, the economic and the natural – cannot be equally true: something has to give. Perhaps these imaginings cloud what is there, obscure the actuality with our prejudices and beliefs, impede any real understanding. Perhaps each is full of truth and half-truth; perhaps none reflect the full reality.

* * *

The aim of this book is not to give each of the four landscapes equal scrutiny: it is instead to rehabilitate the concept of the Highlands as the wild, natural landscape it once was, and not in any way an ecologically degraded or devastated land. I can remember when holidaymakers returning south put a sprig of heather on the bonnet of their cars, the "bonnie purple heather" at that time being a symbol of Scotland. Nowadays, if anyone did this, they could be castigated for being associated with evil landlords who have degraded the landscape by covering the hills with heather for their own ends!

A more appropriate symbol today would be a twig of Scots pine (although I have not seen this yet), that iconic tree named after Scotland and a symbol of the grand restoration now taking place across the land. People forget, or perhaps never knew, that the Scots pine is amongst the commonest of trees in the eastern Palaearctic – the land stretching from Scotland to Vladivostok in the Russian Far East. If it were named the Vladivostok

The Black Isle: once a landscape of moorland and peat bog, now a landscape of farmland and forestry plantation.

pine, would we be so keen on it? It was called "Scots" because in the British Isles in recent centuries it was confined to Scotland. Heather is a much rarer plant globally than the ubiquitous pine; indeed, Scotland is the world centre for the plant: would we value heather more if its official name were "the Scots heather"?

It should be stressed that when here referring to the Highlands as "a wild, natural landscape", this is referring to the 'unimproved' (in farming terms) and uncultivated hill land only, the land above the hill dyke, for of course the inbye land around settlements, the settlements themselves, the western machair, the fertile Moray Firth area and the eastern lowlands have all been heavily modified. This is illustrated on the Black Isle, the peninsula between the Beauly and Cromarty firths, so named because it was once black peatland and moor. Only fragments, such as the Monadh Mor, remain, the rest having been converted to agricultural land and forestry plantation. Such encroachment of agricultural land onto the natural heaths and moors has been particularly common along the eastern foothills and glens of the Highlands, the original landscape often retained only in place names. For example, there is a Muirtown in Inverness, a town today without a vestige of moor within its bounds, and how many 'Mossends' do you know in the agricultural lowlands? And of course forestry plantations have been inserted everywhere.

Because of its physical characteristics, large parts of the Highlands are unsuitable for agricultural improvement and settlement, and it is this land that is the focus of this book. The word 'Highlands' as used here covers the area north of the Highland Boundary Fault, which stretches from the Isle of Arran in the west, through Helensburgh and on to Stonehaven in the east.

The book does not attempt to be a treatise on the history of the Gàidhealtachd (the Highlands and Islands of Scotland), on the Highland people or on the role of landownership. The political landscape has been introduced here to illustrate the current conflation of ecology and politics.[12] This entanglement can so colour one's view that any landscape type associated with the landowning fraternity suffers guilt by association: in many people's eyes because the situation is 'bad' politically, the land must also be bad ecologically! This makes it difficult for evidence to get a foot in the door.

The book aims to eschew politics, does not judge landownership (a complex subject) or land use, but instead concentrates on the land itself – its ecological history, how we humans have shaped it, and its future if current trends continue. The economic landscape does reflect the economic potential of the land for energy and tree harvesting, but the question is, do we want economics to be the sole driving force of the landscape? Would we lose something ineffable if it were?

It is hoped that the book will show what will be lost if the Highland landscape is no longer celebrated as an unspoilt land and as one of the most natural areas remaining in Europe. As a species we tend only to value things once they become rare, for rarity appeals to us. Woodland was once rare in the Highlands, so we valued it. Once it becomes common will we value it less?

The book is not discussing the landscape of the settlements but the hill land beyond, as illustrated in the top half of this picture of Achiltibuie.

Looking north from An Groban, above Gairloch, Wester Ross.

Chapter 2 Celebration

An unspoilt land

A landscape of hill and mountain

When viewed from afar, perhaps from a boat offshore on the western seaboard, all that can be seen of the Highland landscape is its silhouette. Indeed, the word 'landscape' itself may have been derived from the Dutch 'landschap', the land as seen from a ship. Every mountain range is distinctive, even when the detail is missing: the Sutherland hills, each with a random shape rising separately from the rocky plain, are said to have been built when the Gods were young and still practising; the serrated Cuillin ridge is identifiable from all directions and distances; the schizophrenic Sgùrr of Eigg is both long and sloping and sharp and pointed; the smooth lumps of the Cuillin of Rum; the complex muddle of the Rough Bounds;[1] the distant whaleback of Ben Nevis rising above all; the distinctive and eponymous Dutchman's Cap; the southern end of the Long Island subsiding gently below the horizon.[2]

It is a landscape of hill and mountain, of contrast between the jagged west and rounded east, but also a landscape of sweeping plains and moors. The flatlands of Caithness, the smooth hinterland of the Isle of Lewis, the great bowl of Rannoch Moor, the high plains of the Cairngorms. But although a land of contrasts, it is also one of great similarities: it is surprising how uniform is the vegetation, from Shetland to Schiehallion, from St Kilda to Tomintoul, from Arran to Cape Wrath. The same species are found throughout; it is only their relative abundance that changes. Heather is more abundant in the east; cross-leaved heath, flying bent[3] and bog asphodel are more common in the wetter west. Bog cotton grows on all the peats, and deer grass flourishes throughout – the plant that gives the moors their orange glow of autumn. Grasses are dominant where richer soils draw grazing animals, although these areas can always be taken over by bracken at lower altitudes. Trees and woods seem a mere afterthought; they are commonest on sloping glen sides and along coastal fringes. Being surrounded by familiar plants, a Scot can feel at home everywhere.

The low-growing plants never hide the great open vistas, so one never feels shut-in – except on those damp, clingy summer days when the wind has stopped blowing and the midges trap you in your own private hell! This land is not the same as the closed-in lands of Scandinavia, where you can never see beyond the next tree and where you can soon feel a deep claustrophobia and longing to be free. Perhaps this is why the Vikings left to stravaig (wander aimlessly) far from their shores, and perhaps why Scandinavian music and myths can be so gloomy. Think of the monotonous *Tapiola*[4] – music with no beginning and no end, that mirrors the endless forests.

In contrast, the Highlands draw the overseas visitor because of the visibility, the sense of freedom and the open road. As John Buchan wrote, "Come forth, the sky is wide and it is a far cry to the world's end"[5]. Where else in Europe can you get this sense of space in a land varying from grandeur to plainness, from ruggedness to homeliness, where intrusions of the modern world are rare and nature is still in charge?

To celebrate fully the Highland landscape, perhaps it is best to invoke some earlier writers. Lord Cockburn, who as a circuit judge was able to tour Scotland at the taxpayer's expense, had a particularly keen eye as recorded in his book *Circuit Journeys*. Referring to The Rest and Be Thankful, a mountain pass in Argyll which he visited in 1838, he wrote:[6]

> As I stood at the height of the road and gazed down on its strange course both ways, I could not help rejoicing that there was at least one place where railways, canals, and steamers and all these devices for sinking hills and raising valleys, and introducing man and levels, and destroying solitude and nature, would for ever be set at defiance.

And after a journey through Glenmoriston in Inverness-shire to Glen Shiel he wrote:[7]

> I have been told to go and see Glenmoriston almost all my life, and now that I have seen it, I am satisfied that I have never got this advice too strongly… For our first hour the rain checked itself in order to let us see the lower part of the glen in peace. I cannot pay these four wooded miles – where the softness of the birch contrast so naturally with the savage rocky stream – a higher compliment than by saying that they reminded me of some parts of the unrivalled Findhorn, by far the finest of British torrents… As the valley opened and rose, its masses of wood disappeared, though it was long adhered to by sprinklings of fine birch and of noble old, branchy Scotch fir; til at last it was a composition of mountain and of water alone. And it would not be easy to find better specimens of either… There is no cultivation, singularly few inhabitants, not one single seat, scarcely above two farm-houses, and these both towards the lower end, not a village, nothing but mountain and water. And I saw enough to satisfy me that the mountain had everything that rock, precipitousness, and peaked summits could give them. Seen in a fine day it must be a noble range.

The Cuillin of Skye across the sea.

John Buchan was also one who, in his writings, fully appreciated the open Scottish hill, as encapsulated in his short story *Streams of Water in the South*:

> And all around, hills huddled in silent spaces, long brown moors crowned with cairns, or steep fortresses of rock and shingle rising to foreheads of steel-like grey. The autumn blue faded in the far sky-line to white, and lent distance to the furthest peaks... I am an old connoisseur in the beauties of the uplands, but I held my breath at the sight.

Although the above is about his beloved Southern Uplands it could equally apply to the Highlands further north. In his poem *Leap in Smoke* he adds:

> [H]ow still the moorlands lie,
> Sleep-locked beneath the awakening sky!
> The film of morn is silver-grey
> On the young heather, and away,
> Dim distant, set in ribs of hill,
> Green glens are shining ...
> The antique home of quietness ...
> But when the even brings surcease,
> Grant me the happy moorland peace;
> That in my heart's depth ever lie
> That ancient land of heath and sky.

Looking southeast from above Gairloch towards An Groban.

Earlier Gaelic writers were equally laudatory – after all it was their home! Duncan Ban Macintyre wrote in his poem *On Ben Dorain*, a hill in the central Highlands:[8]

> Farewell, ye forests of the heath, hills where the bright day gleams,
> Farewell, ye grassy dells, farewell, ye springs and leaping streams,
> Farewell, ye mighty solitudes, where once I loved to dwell –
> Scenes of my spring-time and its joys – for ever fare you well.

And Kenneth Macleod in his *Island Shieling Song*, wrote:[9]

> On the hillside by the shieling, my Mairi my beloved. Like the white lily floating in the peat hagg's dark waters.

Only those who know the peatlands well, with their dubh lochs of deep black water, will understand fully how the beauty of the water lilies shines like a beacon in this moorland landscape. The moors of the eastern hills can to the outsider appear uniform and monotonous, but to Hugh MacDiarmid in his poem *Scotland small?* they are "Nothing but heather! How marvellously descriptive! And incomplete!"

Stob an Chul-Choire (Aonach Mor) from above Roy Bridge.

Trees in the landscape

Trees and woodlands were rarely mentioned by these earlier writers because in the Highlands they were rare. There were some locations where tracts of woodland persisted, such as Invermoriston, referred to by Lord Cockburn above, Glen Affric, Strathspey and the northern shores of Loch Lomond into Glen Falloch. Their distribution on the mainland was well mapped by General Roy and his team between 1747 and 1752[10] after the Battle of Culloden, that epoch-making event which heralded an era of major landscape change following the break-up of the clan system.

However, because we humans have a general, perhaps atavistic, affinity for trees, the modern conservationist has paid far more attention to woodlands in the Highlands than is commensurate with their overall presence – they naturally cover about five per cent of the uplands but have received ninety-five per cent of the attention, their importance overvalued, the whole landscape now managed for them. This is because there is little understanding of the time-depth associated with the vegetation of the area; much is known of the history of the people but not of the ecology of the region, at least by the laity – although it is there to be found if you seek it hard enough.

Nowadays the restoration of ancient buildings and structures is based on a deep understanding of how they evolved to be what they are today, whereas we are far more cavalier with the landscape. Much land management is now predicated on a simplistic understanding of the vegetation history, or even on myths known to be untrue. The presence of Scandinavia to the east has not helped: this landscape is largely covered in trees, hence, it is believed, the Highlands should be as well.

The Inverasdale Peninsula, west of Loch Ewe, Wester Ross.

A dominant southern perspective

The lack of understanding of Highland ecology can also apply to specialists. Many years ago, when I was coordinating a European Union project on upland grazing, the Commissioner of the EU's Environment Directorate joined us on a field visit to assess the project. He asked why we called vegetation "upland" when it occurred at sea level. In the north, upland vegetation came down to sea level and I gave a complex ecological explanation of why, but remember not being totally convinced by my own arguments! However, as it was something we British ecologists knew to be true, I did not pursue my doubts. After all, "An upland type of climate ... descends to sea level in the cooler northwest."[11]

Many years later, however, I realised that if vegetation is common at sea level it is by definition lowland vegetation. But if the same plants are found in the Pennines they would be described as upland vegetation.

This illustrates how names can be misleading. I have heard that people encountering wood anemone on open moorland claim that the area must once have been wooded because the plant grows in woodland. This is true. But could someone from the north, when encountering the plant in a southern wood conclude equally reasonably that that area was once moorland? In which case, another English name for the plant, windflower, might be a more appropriate one to use; indeed, its Gaelic name is *flùr na gaoithe*, flower of the wind. In practice, there are few if any plants in the Highlands that are restricted to woodlands. Old place names are also used to interpret the history of the landscape, but these can be open to opposite interpretations. For example, the name of the mountain Meall a' Ghiuthais means 'hill of the fir-tree', fir being the Scots word for Scots pine. If there is a place so named in an area without a tree in sight does this mean that woodland was at one time common in the area? Or that it was so rare it warranted a place named after it?

It has taken me a lifetime as a professional ecologist to unlearn what I once thought was fact. I now believe that calling plant communities found at sea level in northern Scotland "upland vegetation" is both confusing and ecologically incorrect – as well as being arrant nonsense (but taken for granted because everyone says it). It is an ecological shorthand that tends to hide the real ecological differences between the north and the south – to mask the truism that lowland vegetation in the north is ecologically distinct from lowland vegetation in the south. I have also had to unlearn the 'fact' that there was once a Great Wood of Caledon, an ancient forest since destroyed by humans.

But the landscape of the Highlands has long suffered from being beholden to southern perspectives: outsiders love coming to the area and telling the people what should happen (was it ever thus?). At first, visitors were nervous or hostile about visiting the Highlands but, as the land became more accessible, it became romanticised in the public imagination; this is demonstrated in how portrayals of the area by visiting artists have changed.[12] Outsiders can bring with them perspectives alien, or at least not suited, to the area's distinctive ecology and ecological history, together with their own cultural baggage: for example, the concepts of biodiversity crisis, ecological restoration and rewilding have been imported unthinkingly from the south. Their voices are loud, and over time even the Highlander begins to believe what they are hearing: a landscape degraded by themselves and their forebears, not enough trees, too many deer, too many sheep, too much burning, damaged peat bogs. But more of this later.

An overview of the ecological history

Postglacial succession

The Earth has a long history of climate change, and geologic timespans have been both much colder and much hotter. We are currently in an era of cold alternating with warm, of expansion of the great ice sheets followed by their retreat, with each warm period, or interglacial, lasting between 15,000 and 20,000 years. We should now be nearing the end of our interglacial, but global warming from all the carbon dioxide we have released back into the atmosphere from buried carbon-rich deposits makes return of the ice sheets unlikely, or perhaps even impossible for the next few million years. Anthropogenic global warming is not solely a bad thing, for we could probably more easily survive a warmer world than a colder one with most of Britain covered by ice. Unfortunately we are warming things up too quickly, not giving most of us, and the species we share the planet with, enough time to adjust, and we will most likely take the warming too far.

Hence we have left the climate cycles of the Pleistocene era, from cold to warm and back to cold again, to enter the new Holocene era of continual warming. In fact, the climate has always varied to some extent within interglacials. For example, the whole of Britain was likely to have become more humid when sea levels rose 6,500 years ago and flooded the land between Britain and mainland Europe – the area known then as Doggerland, which is now underwater and known as Dogger Bank. Becoming an island meant water could circulate around the British Isles and moisture-laden winds could arrive from nearly all directions, keeping the land damp, cool in summer and warm in winter, and increasing the oceanicity of the climate. The Highlands would have become even wetter than they were before, being located on the eastern side of a large ocean. Climate variability has continued into the historical era with, for example, both the Mediaeval Warm Period and the Little Ice Age.

These changes in climate result in changes to vegetation. In early 1900 Osgood Mackenzie saw remains of trees at the bottom of Wester Ross peat bogs and observed:[13]

> To mark the manner in which the climate has changed in different periods since the Creation must always be an interesting subject to the student of nature, ancient or modern, and I cannot help thinking that, if the very lowest strata of some of our peat bogs were carefully examined with the help of the microscope, etc., the botanist and entomologist would, at anyrate, derive information which would give us some approximate idea of their age, and would prove that somewhat different vegetation covered the earth when the peat bogs began to form, and that our country was then the abode of plants and insects (if not still of higher forms of animal

Remains of blown-over Scots pine trees at the base of a peat bog in Wester Ross. The bogwood is at the bottom of the peat, indicating that the location has been treeless in the thousands of years since the trees blew over.

Deciduous woodland in the Highlands, which would have been more common during the mesocratic era.

Woodland has been naturally declining in the Highlands for thousands of years so that in this, the oligocratic phase, open moorland dominates the landscape.

life) which are either very rare or are quite extinct with us now, and what were indigenous plants are becoming extinct from various causes, chiefly, I fancy, the climate.

This observation was prescient, as it foreshadowed the modern science of pollen analysis – palynology – which has used pollen preserved at different levels in peat bogs to develop an understanding of how the vegetation has changed since the Ice Age. An interglacial cycle of vegetation has been identified, which, at least for northwest Europe, can be summarised as follows:[14] in the immediate postglacial period there is a cold, cryocratic phase, followed, as the temperature warms, by a protocratic phase. In this period, shade-intolerant plants, shrubs and trees immigrate and expand rapidly to form widespread species-rich grasslands, scrublands and open woodlands, growing on the fertile soils with low humus content.

Thereafter there is the mesocratic phase during which temperate deciduous woodlands take over the fertile soils and shade out many of the open-ground species. This is followed by the oligocratic phase of forest decline during which open conifer-dominated woods, heathlands and bogs develop on the increasingly infertile soils. Local extinction of nutrient-demanding mesocratic plants occurs, woodlands continue to decline and some protocratic plants expand as a result of decreasing shade. Finally there is a phase of climate cooling, the telocratic phase, which leads back to the next glacial cycle.

In summary the phases are cryocratic—protocratic—mesocratic—oligocratic—telocratic—cryocratic, with maximum woodland cover during the mesocratic phase, followed by natural decline of woodland in the oligocratic phase. These phases have occurred even during interglacials without humans present,[15] so it is a natural process.

In our current interglacial we have now reached the oligocratic phase, during which open-ground habitats expand at the expense of woodland.

Soil leaching

The declining fertility of the soils after the mesocratic phase is caused by thousands of years of perpetual rainfall slowly washing all the goodness out of the soil, a process termed 'leaching'. This makes it too acidic for earthworms, and with no worms there can no longer be any soil mixing; the plant remains form a surface layer of humus distinct from the mineral layers below. This type of unmixed, layered soil is called a 'podsol', as opposed to mixed 'brown earth' soils in which worms are present. To make it even more inhospitable for plants, iron precipitates out at depth, forming an impermeable layer, the iron pan, which isolates plant roots from any minerals below and causes waterlogging of the surface layers. Incidentally, this layer of iron, 'bog iron' as it was called, was sometimes extracted for iron smelting.

Hence it is no wonder the fertility of the landscape has declined over the millennia, from fertile, mixed brown earth soils to acidic podsols. The organic surface layers are, though, a significant store of carbon, generally holding more than an equivalent area of trees.

Thousands of years of leaching by rainfall leads to stratified, unmixed soils. These are characterised by a layer of dark, organic humus at the surface, above a grey, leached, mineral layer. Below this is an impermeable iron pan (dark rust coloured) and then an orange layer, the colour coming from iron (rust). See also Case Study 1 on disturbed soils. The organic surface layers can store more carbon than any trees growing on the site.

Disturbed ground at a construction site: the soil is now a mixture of the original humus layer and the underlying mineral soil, with the iron pan destroyed. The resultant mixed soil has higher fertility, allowing a different range of plants to colonise, including rushes. The original vegetation (brown) is in the background.

This process of soil leaching by rainfall led to the development of forestry ploughing: the plough breaks up the iron pan and brings the more nutrient-rich soil to the surface, allowing trees to thrive. Indeed, disturbance of the soil by human action from a variety of causes is now common across the Highland landscape and, as will be seen in Chapter 4, is having a major impact on the region's ecology: by making nutrients available to plants it returns the landscape from the current oligocratic phase back to the richer mesocratic phase. This can be observed on forestry clear-felled sites where the disturbed ground can result in the abundant regeneration of indigenous trees such as birch, which would be rare or absent on unforested open hill.

The slow reduction of fertility over the millennia inevitably resulted in long-term vegetation change, with acid-loving plants such as heather and bog asphodel taking over from more nutrient-demanding species, resulting in the heaths and acid grasslands we have today. It has also encouraged the spread of peatlands because the more acid soil conditions allow peat-forming plants to colonise and expand at the expense of non-peat-forming ones.[16] In the mesocratic era the soil conditions would have been less suited to these peat-forming species, although peat in some places started forming in hollows almost as soon as the ice retreated.

The above illustrates how the vegetation of the landscape over millennia can naturally change without any associated change in climate.

Natural woodland loss

Pollen that falls on the surface of a peat bog will in time be incorporated in the peat and so can be used to analyse the surrounding vegetation at the time the peat was laid down. It is the results of such pollen analysis that have identified the interglacial succession discussed above. These results support the original view of the famous Scottish geologist James Geikie, who in 1867 stated that "It can be shown that the destruction of our ancient forests has not been primarily due to man."[17] In other words there has been a natural decline of woodland from a postglacial maximum in the mesocratic phase.

Geikie based his conclusion on his study of the remains of trees found at the base of Scottish peat bogs. Hillwalkers will be familiar with the bleached stumps of Scots pine in peat bogs across Scotland, which are normally exposed as the peat erodes. However, these mostly represent a period of maximum woodland cover and are normally 4,000 to 6,000 years old. It is perhaps surprising that such tree remains are rare or absent in peat less than 4,000 years old: if woodland had remained common in the landscape, you would expect to find bog woodland at all levels in the peat, but this is rarely the case.

Based on pollen evidence, the researcher Paterson says that ancient woods began to fragment as early as 7,500 years ago, although the actual date of decline varied from place to place and began earliest in the west.[18] He suggests that, although human activity is sometimes implicated in woodland fragmentation, this may only have reinforced what would happen naturally in a maritime climate. According to Birks, in the Loch Maree area where woodland is rare, the dominant open heath and bog have been around for the past 4,000 years with human impact minimal.[19]

At the Great Britain level, Fyfe has reviewed the evidence from pollen analysis on the openness or otherwise of British vegetation and concluded:[20]

> At the continental scale, western Atlantic Europe has for long been more open than other parts of the mainland. Britain and Ireland (especially western and northern regions) are particularly notable in this context, and are different from much of inland continental Europe. This conclusion is replicated irrespective of which analytical method is applied to the pollen data.

It is important to note that as the woodland naturally declined in the Highlands the animals associated with it would have declined also – red squirrels, capercaillie and lynx

The remains of a large Scots pine at the base of a peat bog in Wester Ross. This stump is likely to be between 5,000 and 6,000 years old. Much of the vertical face of peat is hidden by overhanging heather.

Isolated woodland is characteristic of the Highlands. Pictured are the northern slopes of Ben Shieldaig, Wester Ross.

The Highland building tradition was previously of turf and stone because trees were generally rare in the region in the past.

– sometimes to extinction, because there was not enough of their habitat left. In contrast, more adaptable animals such as red deer and fox have survived the woodland loss, and the wolf would have as well if it had not been hunted to extinction. The red deer is often perceived as a woodland animal, particularly because it mainly occurs in woodland elsewhere in Europe. But it can easily survive on the open hill of the Highlands, although this may result in the animals being smaller than those living in sheltered woodland.

This is not to say that there has been no human destruction of the forest, whether by burning, felling or livestock grazing but, in the grand order of things, this would be localised and have merely accelerated the natural decline of the woods, or at least thinned them out. Some of this destruction is discussed by the historian Christopher Smout in his book *Nature Contested*.[21] However, it is easy to erroneously generalise such local destruction to the whole Highland landscape. The woods would be expected to regenerate naturally after such events if conditions were ecologically suitable, as noted later on p. 32.

The absence or rarity of woodland in the Highlands is reflected in the building traditions of the area. Most houses historically, at least for the average clansman, were built of turf and were absorbed back into the ground when abandoned. Stone houses later came to dominate, perhaps starting with Stone Age structures such as those at Skara Brae in Orkney and succeeded by Bronze Age roundhouses with a stone base, Norse longhouses, Pictish brochs, the thatched, round-cornered black houses and finally the white-washed but and ben cottages which, with the larger, more pretentious houses for the tacksmen or farmers, have been so characteristic of the Highlands in the last century or so.

The white houses and bigger farmhouses that post-dated Culloden were built to a standard pattern but, compared to what they had replaced, were cold and draughty, an unfortunate tradition in Scottish housing that persists to this day. However, the new houses showed that the Highlands were entering the modern world,[22] although their construction ignored the fact that the traditional black houses were more suited to the environment: they had no chimney through which heat could escape, small windows and the warmth provided by livestock nearby. In modern terms we would say the black houses were energy efficient. The clan chiefs, with labour to support them, built large castles, many of which are now romantic ruins loved by tourists. But away from the heat of the kitchen range they also must have been cold and damp for much of the year. This was perhaps illustrated by the composer Chopin who, on a visit to Scotland, complained of the eternal indoor cold he encountered. Maybe it contributed to the Scots being seen as hardy.

The Scottish building tradition contrasts with that of Scandinavia, where timber has always been plentiful and wood the building material of choice. It is from where Scotland has imported its timber, there having been a long tradition of trade with the Baltic states. Wood was so rare in parts of the Highlands that timber joists were part of dowries for weddings on the Long Island, a situation unimaginable in Norway.

The impact of grazing

The decline of woods in the oligocratic phase is partly due to changing soil conditions but also to grazing animals. In places with optimum soil conditions tree seedlings will colonise open ground and grow quickly, their sheer numbers enabling some to escape being eaten by red deer. Their rapid growth means they are above browsing height within two or three years, and so woodland can survive and prosper. Where soil conditions are poorer, though, there will be fewer seedlings and saplings in the first place and they will take longer to grow above browsing height, say ten years, and there is more chance that all will be eaten. This would explain Svenning's conclusion that the presence of large herbivores would have more impact on infertile soils such as those of the Highlands:[23]

> Vegetation development during the preceding [pre-Holocene] interglacials ... suggests that open woodland or even heath vegetation can develop on nutrient-poor soils. Numerous interglacials show expanding non-tree percentages ... This development is interpreted as caused by acid, infertile soil conditions and perhaps increasing rainfall ... The ability of large herbivores to open up the vegetation would probably also be stronger on poor soils.

In practice, the same level of grazing can have different impacts in different places. Along the mild coastal fringes there is likely to be some grass growth throughout the winter; here, grazing animals such as sheep and deer will preferentially graze the more nutritious grasses than any tree saplings, allowing woodland to persist. In the west, low altitude woodlands are currently regenerating, but in the hills away from the coast there is no grass growth in winter to support the animals, so trees and their buds, even if of low nutritional value, will all be eaten. This helps explain the rarity of woods in the Scottish uplands and their relative abundance along the coastal fringe, even in areas of human settlement.

In other parts of the world, such as Boreal Scandinavia and the European Alps, winter snow cover prevents the young trees from being eaten; in areas of lowland Europe ecologically suited to thorny shrubs such as hawthorn, blackthorn and bramble, these can protect young trees from grazing.[24] But Highland soils are mostly too acidic for these shrubs. This, and little consistent winter snow cover, explains why the landscape is naturally likely to become more open and treeless as the interglacial period progresses from mesocratic to oligocratic.

Grazing animals have always been an integral part of most terrestrial ecosystems, with the animals in large enough numbers to support the range of carnivores that used to be present across Europe. When people in Scotland say "There are too many deer", this is mainly because deer eat trees and people think that trees should be present; it is not related to the normal ecological principle of how many animals the land can support.[25] In Europe we are not used to seeing a profusion of wild animals

Red deer on Islay.

Woodland would naturally be more common along the coastal fringe because the milder conditions in winter mean trees are less likely to be eaten by browsing animals.

Grazing by indigenous herbivores, here a red deer is a natural feature of most terrestrial ecosystems. It helps shape the landscape.

and so tend to see their rarity as the norm, forgetting that we have taken over their land, making many species extinct in the process. Instead we travel on safari to the plains of Africa to enjoy the vast herds. Perhaps, within Europe, only in the Scottish Highlands has there been a significant population of an indigenous large herbivore, the red deer, throughout the postglacial period: there was always space for them in the wild, uncultivated Highlands, large tracts of which were unused by people and left to themselves.

The red deer is an endangered species in the Caucasus, but not in the Highlands. Is this not a conservation success story for Scotland, albeit by default? And are deer not part of the landscape, not something to be reduced to a mere rarely seen rump? Instead there seems to be a belief amongst Highland conservationists, which has now infiltrated the public at large, that numbers of grazing animals should be low, "in balance with woodland" is the phrase, and that they should not be damaging the vegetation. But a grazing animal cannot survive without damaging some plant or other. It is just that, owing to our affinity with trees, we do not like them to be eaten.

But think of Europe way back in the Stone Age when there was a much greater array of herbivores in the landscape. As well as red and roe deer, there would have been bison, elk and wild boar, and the now extinct aurochs, tarpan (wild horse) and Irish elk:[26] these, surely, would have impacted the vegetation pattern, in spite of the presence of the wolf, brown bear and lynx. In America, what about the huge herds of buffalo that once roamed the prairies? And going back to the Mesozoic period, surely the massive dinosaurs, in size and perhaps also in herds, must have played a major role in establishing the pattern of vegetation. So why, today, do we think that the grazing impact should be minimal or zero? Is it purely because we want trees back in the landscape? In which case, in the Highlands, we are fighting the natural ecological succession to open moor described above – which is why it is so difficult to get trees back: the soils need to be optimised through disturbance, sometimes with the addition of fertilisers, and animals must be excluded using industrially-produced fence wire, or reduced in numbers to way below any natural level.

Nowadays, conservation organisations in Scotland talk of expanding woodlands through reducing grazing and allowing the subsequent 'natural regeneration'; but how can such regeneration be natural when a whole trophic level – the grazing aspect intrinsic to nearly all ecosystems – is virtually eliminated, made functionally extinct? Ultimately there is enough food in the landscape to maintain grazing animals at a number much higher than the extremely low level necessary to give trees any chance of surviving. It is not surprising, therefore, that the Highland landscape is largely open. Perhaps this is too simple a concept for most people to accept.

Instead the word 'overgrazing' is today bandied around even though the concept is weak and needs to be used with caution. As the scientist Jos Milner and her team conclude in a study of deer populations on the Letterewe Estate of Wester Ross:[27]

> Overgrazing is a controversial term ... Its precise definition is dependent on management objectives ... Overgrazing is not generally applied to natural ecosystems, even under heavy grazing pressure, because wild herbivores are regulated by their food supply during the unfavourable season ... For example, there is no evidence of habitat degradation on St Kilda or the North Block of Rum where herbivore populations are naturally regulated.

Because people have made that top carnivore, the wolf, extinct in Scotland, it is argued that we now have too many deer. If only the wolf were brought back then all would be well. But 10,000 years of Highlands history shows that this is unlikely to be the case: the wolf became extinct around 1700, whereas the Roy Maps show us that the woods had largely long gone by then.[28] In other words, the woods declined during the thousands of years when wolves were still present.

On a similar theme, others have pointed out that it is not necessarily the case that the presence of predators will significantly reduce the numbers of grazing animals. For example, Ian Macleod writes:[29]

> The important factors are the climate and food available. If you looked at the savannah of Africa and saw a herd of 10,000 wildebeest walking across, and in the foreground there was a pride of lions, you would instinctively recognise the lions cannot control these numbers. It's grass and water that do that.

It is not only in Africa that this situation of large herbivores keeping the landscape open occurs. The environmental historian Jed Kaplan says that removal of large animal species by humans has had effects on the landscape that are apparent almost everywhere:[30]

> A lot of land would be semi-open, kept partly open by these big herds of grazers and browsers and predators. It is important to keep in mind that landscape is also shaped by animals. These giant herds of bison would be trampling down little trees and keeping the landscape open.

What is meant by biodiversity?

The modern world has developed its interest in nature conservation just in time to catch the natural endpoint of Highland woods. The remaining woods have become rare and, so the thinking goes, being rare they are valuable and (a non-sequitur) more must be better. The word 'endpoint', however, is an exaggeration because it is probable that some woods will remain. Additionally, ecology is a statistical science, lacking universal or absolute truths: generally, exceptions can be found to any dogmatic ecological statement.

Woods are likely to persist in locations inaccessible to grazing animals and in other sites suited to tree regeneration such as coastal slopes and steep glen sides at lower altitudes. It is even possible to conceive of the woodland cover naturally expanding again if the climate becomes more optimal for trees, particularly if this results in drier soil conditions. But a characteristic of the Highland landscape must be one of isolated and fragmented woodland, in effect a 'biodiversity characteristic' of the area. The word 'biodiversity' is often used but rarely defined and in practice means all things to all people. Biodiversity is a useful concept but folk are perhaps misdirected by the 'diversity' part of it. They confuse 'biodiversity' with 'maximum diversity', that is, having as many plants and animals around as possible. There is a scale issue: many of us want to conserve the biodiversity of the planet, to conserve its full, rich panoply of plants and animals. However, each corner of the planet has a different array of species: some areas are not diverse and poor in species, whereas others have a much richer array. At a global scale, conserving biodiversity means conserving the natural ecological characteristics of every region, some rich in plants and animals and some poor. With this definition, 'biodiversity' is a given – it cannot be increased, although it can be restored if lost or damaged. Hence biodiversity conservation can mean keeping some landscapes species-poor: adding species to them will in fact reduce global diversity by removing their natural characteristics.

The Highlands are particularly poor in species for several reasons: from being on an island – islands are always more species-poor than continents owing to the problem of colonisation across water; and from being on the northern fringe of Britain where soils are infertile and the climate more extreme. The region is a difficult place for animals and plants so has limited flora and fauna, which is why the same vegetation is found from Shetland to the Mull of Kintyre: only a few specialist plants can survive. There are exceptions of course (there always are in ecology): the humid climate makes the Highlands a world centre for mosses, liverworts and lichens, plants which most people

There is nothing unnatural about the restriction of woods to places grazing animals find hard to reach, such as crags, steep slopes, gullies and islands – here illustrated in Glen Coe. It is a biodiversity characteristic of the Highlands.

Relict native woods can be beautiful places but it is a mistake in conservation terms to use this appeal to justify making this kind of wood more common. Here Coille na Glas Leitire, Wester Ross.

fail to notice. But as for trees, forget them! The Highlands is not a world centre, although it is rarely recognised that it is for moorland plants such as heather, cross-leaved heath and bog asphodel.

The terrestrial biodiversity of the Highlands, therefore, is characterised by the vegetation of unwooded moorland, itself a mosaic of dry heather moor, wet heathland, peat bog and grasslands, which is mostly poor in the number of plants species but sometimes rich. Its isolated woodlands can be species rich or species poor, and the woodlands themselves vary depending on which of the native trees dominates, whether oak, birch, ash, alder, willow or Scots pine; Scotland has only a limited range of trees to choose from. Nonetheless, these relict woods can be beautiful and entrancing places, albeit difficult to wander through without a path.

Open moorland dominates the landscape because its vegetation is the most resilient to the varying ecological pressures it has faced over the millennia, whether climate variability, soil deterioration or grazing animals; it would be absent today if it were not. Woodland, in contrast, is not resilient, being particularly susceptible to changing soil conditions and grazing. Hence it is not common. Moorland is also likely to be resilient in a warming world because there are few other plants capable of colonising its specialist environment. The exception is the ability of certain introduced trees and shrubs to colonise, and even dominate, moorland vegetation at the expense of native plants, in particular rhododendron and Sitka spruce; additionally, moorland plants cannot withstand major ground disturbance, but more about this in Chapter 4.

A landscape of peat

Scotland is of course renowned for its peat bogs and is indeed a 'world centre' for peatland. Peat, the accumulation of undecayed plant remains, is found in many forms across the world, from the frozen bogs of the Arctic tundra to extensive coastal tropical swamps. In the British Isles, three main types can be found:[31] valley peatlands are damp hollows and basins filled with peat, their extent constrained by topography; on coastal flats and on flat lowland glen floors, peat can build up in an unconstrained manner resulting in extensive dome-shaped 'raised bogs' such as the coastal flows and mosses that once surrounded the Solway Firth, although only a few of these mosses now remain; the third type of peatland, which is very similar to raised bogs, is 'blanket peat', so termed because it blankets the whole landscape. This type is restricted to cool, humid climates. The Highlands have some of the most extensive blanket peatlands in the world, the prime exemplar being the Flow Country of Caithness and Sutherland.

In landscapes where peat is common, the distinction between the three types can become blurred. Raised bogs and blanket peat are unique in that they can defy gravity and rise above the ground, obvious to anyone who has seen peat-cuttings in the crofting counties. This peat can reach three metres in height, possible because the densely packed plant remains hold water; in technical terms upward capillary movement of water in the peat is a stronger force than gravitational drainage.[32] The water is in effect stuck in the peat and supports the whole structure. The exposed face of a peat-cutting does not collapse, nor does its water drain out. Plant roots in these bogs cannot penetrate down to the mineral soil underneath so the only nutrients plants can get must come from rainfall. Rainfall is not nutrient-rich, making peatlands a specialist environment called 'oligotrophic', in which only a restricted range of plants is able to survive. The low nutrient status of these plants means they are not very popular with grazing animals.

A bog pool in Wester Ross.

The Flow Country of Caithness and Sutherland: a landscape of peat. Looking northeast from Creag Creagach, near Ben Armine Lodge, Sutherland.

The far-reaching Highland bogs may seem dull and monotonous to those who do not know them, but, to quote again Hugh MacDiarmid: "How marvellously descriptive! And incomplete!". Those who have tramped the expanse of mosses will notice the white bog cotton rippling in the breeze, the restrained reds of *Sphagnum* mosses, the rich russets of the autumnal dying, the white water lily in the peat hagg's dark waters, the peat haggs – themselves, a fantastic mess of gully and dark cliff, the bottomless pools that are home to the dragonfly, the call of the pipit and the wader above the sound of the wind. They may be difficult to walk across but they are safe enough if you know where to put your foot, if you can read the bog.

These bogs are fascinating, their time-depth apparent if you look closely. Ancient bogs eventually succumb to erosion and decay, but wait a thousand years and they will grow again, smooth for the first few millennia, then breaking up into gullies and pools, the pools themselves eventually draining away.[33] It is an endless cycle, only stopped by the next ice age.

Why is the full life cycle of these bogs not appreciated more? Young, uniform bogs are seen as boring and dull, miles and miles of nothing, and eroding bogs do not seem interesting because everyone knows that erosion must be wrong and bad and obviously caused by humans. It is only in the mid-phase of their lives that bogs are seen as interesting, when they have the widest diversity of features – when they have a pattern of ridges, hummocks and pools, the latter home to underwater creatures and attractive to birds, and a greater array of plants. But the pools grow bigger, coalesce and eventually drain to become haggs. But surely even peat haggs are endlessly fascinating places. Do they not add unique variety to the Highland landscape?

And of course people could not have survived in this treeless landscape of highlands and islands without peat which, when dried, was used for cooking and heating. Such was the demand that peat ran out on the island of Mingulay, which must have contributed

to the island's eventual evacuation. It probably ran out on St Kilda too, and on Eriskay people had to burn turf because no peat was left; Fair Isle was only saved by the arrival of coal, oil and wind. Today, it is used to fire the distillation the aromatic, smoky, peat-flavoured whiskies, perhaps the best of all.

The history of the Highland landscape is not so much about the loss of woods through human activity as about the loss of the peatlands. Indeed, the extensive peatlands of the Flow Country in Caithness and Sutherland may reflect how much of lowland Scotland would look today if the area had never been farmed. A hint of this can be seen in place names, the Moss-sides, the Muirends, the Bogmuirs and similar, and in a few places relicts of these once-great bogs still exist, such as Auchenforth Moss south of Penicuik and Flanders Moss west of Stirling.

Eroding peatlands are fascinating places. Blanket peat does not live for ever, instead going through millennial-scale cycles of growth and erosion.

Human impact before the Battle of Culloden of 1746

The Battle of Culloden fought in 1746 on Culloden's eponymous moor was epoch-making. Moorlands, particularly Britain's lowland heaths, were often chosen as battlefields because of their open and uncluttered nature, which offered plenty of room for troop manoeuvrings.[34] Recent thinking suggests that lowland heaths throughout western Europe are not, as often thought, cultural landscapes created through tree felling and livestock grazing, but instead are descendants of grazing-dependent natural ecosystems, naturally occurring open landscapes in locations of infertile soil.[35] They include in England areas such as the Breckland and Dorset heaths, and probably the high Pennine moors. In other words, their origin is similar to the open Highland landscapes, although nowadays they have a greater cultural overlay. Indeed, a large percentage of the British flora and fauna is dependent on open-ground habitats, indicating that unwooded ground must have always been common.

But back to Culloden. The battle marked the opening of the Highlands to the outside world: roads, largely absent before, were built thereafter and the world could flood in, bringing with it concepts of land management previously alien to the Gaelic culture, particularly the idea that land was there to provide pecuniary income to its owner. Before Culloden, although land surrounding settlements – the inbye land – had always been intensively worked to provide food, the remainder was largely left to itself, apart from summer grazing on the best ground through the practice of transhumance (seasonally

A glen in Torridon which has never been populated, albeit with one old shieling site on an alluvial fan.

moving livestock from one area to another), the harvesting of peat and, where present, of wood. It was also a source of wild meat, particularly venison, grouse and salmon, at least for the higher echelons of Gaelic society. But most of the hill land was largely unused and uncared for; it had no particular use, apart, perhaps, from the royal forests, which were appropriated as hunting grounds and excluded other people. The word 'forest', in this context, meant unmanaged land.

But the hill land has always been largely unpopulated, as explained by the noted Scottish historian Tom Devine:[36]

Settlement in the western Highlands and Islands was mainly confined to very limited areas because of the challenging constraints of geology, climate and geography. Therefore, when modern visitors contemplate hills and glens which are empty of people, they should not assume they were inhabited in the past.

And Haldane states:[37]

When cross-country droving in Scotland on an appreciable scale first began, and for many a year thereafter, a great part of the Highland and upland areas of the country was common land, or at the least land which, while nominally owned by the local chieftain, was in fact unused and uncared for. In the earliest rentals for Islay and Kintyre ... the figures representing the total of the 'merk lands' held by the tacksmen from the local chieftains do not amount to more than about one-third of the total extent of these areas as shown on modern maps. The rest was wasteland which was gradually merged into the tacksmen's holdings with the progress of agriculture ... not until sheep farming on a large scale became common in the Highlands were these upland areas put to fuller use than for the grazing of cattle from the shielings in summer and early autumn.

To some extent the wrong impression of population density is gained when driving along many Highland roads today because these tend to follow the long-populated straths and glens, which are not typical of the wider landscape. Of course certain locations have been inhabited by people since soon after the last glaciers disappeared, particularly along the coastal fringe, where first hunter-gatherers, and later, farmers settled. The land in the west is not well suited to arable farming, so most farming has been livestock grazing, as exemplified by the droving trade, which was taking place well before Culloden. This involved driving cattle south from the Highlands to markets in central Scotland and England.[38]

It is possible to envisage in earlier times the impact of humans on the landscape, where there are two possible contrasting scenarios: the destruction of woodland through felling and burning, or its expansion through reduced grazing as a result of deer hunting. However, environmental historian Richard Tipping tells us:[39]

Peat-cuttings, old and new, covering a landscape of blanket peat on Shetland.

> Hunter-gatherers before 4,000 BC are often thought to have modified the woodland cover
> but evidence for substantial alteration is hard to find … Human impacts in later prehistory
> remained limited, with no real acceleration of human activities. Clearance was still small in
> scale and always followed by woodland regeneration.

It cannot be said, though, that the human population in the later eras before Culloden
had no influence on the landscape: there will have been locations around settlements
where people destroyed woodland, managed woodland or planted woodland. But overall
woodland was rare.

Where human impact is more certain is in the destruction of peat bogs, and this
can easily be observed: the straight edge of old peat-cuttings now distant from any
habitation, the empty hollows, the bare rock and barren stony ground so common in
many places. Peat was also dug for export to the energy-guzzling towns, from Orkney to
Edinburgh for example, and there is even a report of ten tonnes of peat being exported
to Australia.[40] Why has this destruction received so little attention compared to the
destruction of the woods?

The exception is Shetland and Orkney, where the loss of peat over the centuries has
been described by the renowned ethnographer Sandy Fenton in his book *The Northern
Isles*.[41] For example, the island of North Ronaldsay in Orkney now comprises good-
quality agricultural grassland whereas it was once peat-covered. As the centuries went
by and the peat eventually ran out, some islands such as Graemsay had to import it from
neighbouring islands. On Papa Stour in Shetland the lack of peat resulted in depopulation,
and it had already disappeared by 1683 from Dunrossness and The Skerries.

Celebration

In summary, the open, unwooded nature of the Highlands can easily be explained without invoking human involvement. But, because there is so much destruction to the natural environment in the world today, including the destruction of forests, we assume it applies everywhere; we unthinkingly apply it to the Highlands without trying to understand the ecological history of the area, which is different to that of other parts of Britain and mainland Europe. Humans destroyed the forest, so humans must put it back, a neat story and in keeping with the spirit of the age. But what if we have got this all wrong? Are we not in danger of damaging a unique corner of the world?

It is not as if the importance of this unwooded land has not been acknowledged. Its heathlands, peat bogs and some of its grasslands are recognised as being of international importance under the Habitats Directive, legislation that was strongly promoted by British conservationists in the 1980s to ensure legal protection for Europe's biodiversity. Now that Britain has left the European Union, will its interests revert to parochial concerns, the wider international perspective being lost? This certainly appears to be the case in Scotland where, with the exception of peatlands, conservationists seem determined to replace much of the Highlands' rare vegetation with something more common.

But what if the Highlands do represent one of the most natural landscapes remaining in Europe, having survived the vicissitudes of human endeavour, escaped the plough and being managed for trees, escaped being managed at all? Is attempting to make it more wild by planting trees, which 'rewilding' means to many, instead making it less wild, forcing it into our image of what should be there, destroying the unbroken link to the Ice Age, converting it from a natural landscape to a designed landscape? Should biodiversity conservation not be about safeguarding a region's natural characteristics? For the biodiversity of an area is a given. It can be restored if damaged, but it cannot be added to, for then the restoration site becomes artificial, a land created by us rather than by nature. We would not take a Van Gogh or a Rembrandt and restore it if damaged by slapping paint over it; we would first subject it to meticulous historical research. Why then do we not do the same with our valuable Highland landscapes? Why are we so cavalier?

Looking towards the Isle of Rum from the Isle of Muck.

Sròn na Gaoithe from Glas Maol, above Glenshee.

The little known European Landscape Convention,[42] to which Scotland is a signatory, aims to prevent the homogenisation of landscapes, that is, to prevent everywhere looking the same. There is a danger that we are forcing our hill land to become more like the European norm. An oft-quoted figure shows that Scotland has far less woodland than the European average and is used to justify increasing the country's tree cover. Even the new woods are standardised, with a checklist of native trees and the amount of open ground to include. In spite of the Convention we are homogenising the landscape and the detail within it. Nature is not getting a look-in.

The argument that we must change the landscape because it does not match the European average does not bear scrutiny. France has less blanket peat than the European average, Italy less heather moorland, Norway greater glacier cover. Should these countries be trying to homogenise themselves? Making everywhere look the same indicates a lack of understanding of the sciences of geography, geology and ecology. Additionally, we have a tendency to create landscapes appealing to ourselves, that achieve a 'balance' of open ground and woodland. Jay Appleton explains that as hunter-gatherers we liked trees near us to hide in but also open ground from which to espy danger.[43] We have carried this over to the present day and are creating a land appealing to ourselves, with nature only allowed to survive if it appeals or is useful.

Similarly, nature conservation bodies use appealing animals such as red squirrels in their marketing, despite the species nearly becoming extinct in the Highlands as its woodland habitat declined and fragmented. In some cases woodland extinction may have been hastened by us, but, without the extensive reintroductions across the Highlands since the 1800s,[44] the red squirrel's ultimate fate in the region could well have been natural extinction. Recently created forest means there is potential for more squirrels but does that turn nature conservation from the conservation of natural habitats and species into large-scale zookeeping? Because much forest loss elsewhere in the world has been caused by humans does not mean that the same applies to the Highlands.

Strathspey, west of the Cairngorms, has managed to retain more Scots pine woodland than elsewhere over the centuries, perhaps because, being furthest from the sea, it has a more continental and less oceanic climate than elsewhere, which is more suited to the pine. But the situation is complicated because the presence of the River Spey means that it has always been possible to float logs down to the sea, for example for shipbuilding at Speymouth on the Moray coast. This export trade has given the timber a value it did not originally have elsewhere, where export was not possible on any scale. Hence there is a much longer history of timber management in Strathspey than in most other parts of the Highlands, which could result in both more forest being present than would naturally be there, through management and planting, or less through timber extraction. To a lesser extent, in the eighteenth and nineteenth centuries the rivers Ness and Dee were also used to float down timber to support the then flourishing shipbuilding industry.[45] But native woodland is still common along the shores of Loch Ness and associated side glens, so this did not destroy all the woodland. The situation is complex and difficult to untangle.

It is not an aim of this book to look at each area of the Highlands and discuss its woodland history. Instead its aim is to establish broad principles to explain why most of the area is treeless, with the same dominant plants found throughout – which are not trees!

So let us celebrate the Highland landscape as we find it, not be cross with it for what it is not! Let us give thanks that there is still a part of the world, even in heavily populated Europe, where nature still rules the roost, which has never been planned, managed or modified, where you can still visit and understand how nature works. This is important

Ben Dearg from the south (above Braemore, Wester Ross). Let us celebrate our open landscapes.

Beinn Alligin, Torridon, Wester Ross.

because if everywhere is managed we will forget this, forget that before we humans came along nature managed to get on very well on its own. Well, perhaps not so very well at times, when meteors struck, or the world became too hot or too cold, but at least it survived!

The Highland landscape has got by for over 10,000 years without our help. Does it suddenly need it now? Maybe, to return animals we knowingly made extinct (and whose habitat would still remain), such as the beaver, the sea eagle and the polecat and, dare I mention it, the wolf; and to remove the plants foreign to our shores which are slowly taking over. Otherwise, we should let it be. Does it really matter if heath is converting to grassland or grassland to heath, if woodlands are coming or going, if peat bogs are growing or eroding? Nature has not previously worried about this, so why should we?

Would the Highlands not be a better place if we could instead remove the miles and miles of fencing that prevents movement, compartmentalises everything and is aesthetically horrible? It compartmentalises our minds also, so that we see the landscape in fragments, not the whole.

Let us celebrate the grand vistas over mountain and moor, the bare-boned, inaccessible hills, the complexity, colours and extent of the peatlands, the complex archipelagos of the western seaboard. Let us celebrate the time-depth, the unbroken link back to a period when ice sheets obscured all but the highest tops joining the whole together. Let us celebrate an open land, stark and unforgiving, the backdrop to whole histories and site of conflicts between clan and clan, clan and invader or clan and king or church, a land that has shaped Highland culture and, owing to the writings of Walter Scott, the culture of Scotland itself. Les us celebrate the great herds of deer in their corries or the red grouse at home in the heather. Let us celebrate the heather itself.

Do this and we will no longer demean the land or remove its last vestiges of wildness or force it to suffer the same fate as elsewhere, humans in charge of all. Ochone, ochone....

Chapter 3 Lamentation

Critique

The push for trees

If the landscape is so pure and unsullied, why is there so much desire to change it? I can just remember when you could drive across the watershed of Scotland from west to east or east to west and not see a single fence, forest plantation, hill track or other signs of human intrusion; only the great sweeps of untrammelled wildness were visible, as described so evocatively by Lord Cockburn. Now the land is filling up with our interventions, it seems that on every new trip along a Highland road another hillside has gone, another glen swamped, another section compartmentalised by wires, another burn piped, another road bulldozed up the hill. Even visible from that main artery, the A9 trunk road, the land has been ploughed for the benefit of trees, the open heathland gone, destroyed by a practice which should have been outlawed long ago.

Forestry ploughing of land is the terrestrial kin of that much castigated practice of scallop-dredging at sea. Ploughing up the seabed or ploughing up the land: both destroying everything in their paths, although forestry ploughing is worse because to some extent the dredged seabed can quickly recover. The forest plough is indifferent to the land: lines must be straight, no matter what the archaeology, the vegetation, the risk of flooding or the impact on the climate.[1] I have often wondered what the

Forestry ploughing of moorland west of the A9 trunk road at Dalnamein.

Relict lazy beds on the island of Vatersay. The ridges and furrows will be visible for thousands of years although, unlike forestry ploughing, they do not cover whole landscapes.

person in the tractor must be thinking: pleased with a job well done, supporting the local economy, unhappy about the destruction caused, or indifferent? Why is there not more outcry? For this is permanent scarring, the regular stripes remaining there for all to see even if the trees are long gone. It is a permanent artificiality, in the way that lazy beds (a traditional ridge-and-furrow form of cultivation) can still be seen long after they are no longer used. However, the lazy beds are localised and tell a story of human endeavour. They do not indicate the destruction of a whole landscape.

It is easy to see why the double mouldboard forest plough was invented, and needed a caterpillar tractor to drag it through the soil: it breaks the iron pan, brings mineral soil to the surface and allows drainage, all things that help trees grow well and all allow the landscape to revert to the mesocratic phase of more fertile soils and higher tree cover. Nowadays the less damaging practice of mounding is often used instead – that is, creating hollows and dollops with a digger instead of continuous plough lines; it is certainly more sensitive to the landscape, but it still destroys the naturalness of the soils and releases carbon.

The much-maligned pattern of landownership aids our desire to add trees to the landscape. Great tracts of land can be acquired to create blanket commercial forestry and to sate the need for large-scale visionary things such as rewilding whole landscapes, recreating the Great Forest of Caledon or, most recently, carbon offsetting through tree planting. Organisations and individuals can buy up the land to fulfil their dreams without having to negotiate with hundreds of individual smallholders. Those involved are not much interested in the history of the landscape and have no understanding of time-depth. Questioning their approach is akin to challenging religious beliefs. They have excellent marketing skills, the broadcast and written media are sympathetic and uncritical, and everyone knows that the woodland lobby is on the side of the angels.

There are two strong cohorts of interest pushing for the Highlands, indeed Scotland as a whole, to be covered with trees. Firstly the commercial sector, supported by government, promotes the need for productive conifer forests, mostly of North American Sitka spruce. The claim that this supports the economy is conflated with that of trees being necessary to counteract global warming. Secondly there is the conservation sector, which wants to recreate a long-lost ecological Garden of Eden, a garden that has withered over the centuries owing to gross misuse of the land, particularly the loss of its trees and its putative treeline.

The whole forestry or woodland lobby has become a juggernaut, comprising the government, with its own agency dedicated to trees,[2] the commercial timber sector, the conservation organisations, the sycophantic media, and the public who go with the flow. The open hill suffers because there has never been a government-backed body representing moorland to balance the forestry lobby – no lobby then or now to stand up for the open hill. Its only backers seem to be certain landowners and sheep farmers, but both of these groups are seen as not in keeping with modern times: the landowners because they want to keep the land for their own pursuits, and sheep farmers because sheep are a bad thing, damaging the land and being composed of meat which we should no longer be eating. But are sheep not reared extensively on the hill, with minimal input of anything? And is not their wool organic, made of non-plastic fibres that do not pollute the planet? And is any methane they, and hill cattle, generate produced from recycled grass rather than fossil fuels, causing no net increase in atmospheric carbon?

It is as if there is a great overwhelming mass of blancmange pushing the Highlands in one direction. Attempting to change its direction seems futile. However, many forestry lobby arguments do not bear scrutiny, as discussed in the next section.

The green shoots of a new woodland of native Scots pine on heather at Dava Moor in Moray. Heather moorland is a rarer habitat globally than Scots pine forest.

Analysis of current approaches to conservation in the Highlands

The following sections describe the claims used to underpin much of the landscape change taking place in the Highlands. Below each heading is a summary of the argument, followed by a critique.

Restoring the Great Wood of Caledon

There was once a great forest that cloaked the Highland landscape, but it has been destroyed by humans over the centuries and it needs to be re-created in the name of 'ecological restoration'.

The rationale of commercial forestry is economic but why has the conservation lobby become so obsessed with clothing the Highlands in trees, peatland excepted? In 1867 Geikie stated that "the destruction of our ancient forests has not been primarily due to man"[3] but this has been transmogrified into the modern imperative of restoring a long-lost forest destroyed by humans and their animals. It is common to read in the literature of conservation organisations that they are restoring such a forest.

The concept of the Caledonian Forest began centuries ago, being marked on Ptolemy's map of Scotland from about AD100 as 'Caledonia silva'. This is a crude map seen through modern eyes but it does show the centre of northern Scotland as wooded, although recent historians argue that this map is misleading. David Breeze states:[4]

> Roman descriptions do not allow the forest to be located with any exactitude; the sceptic might even doubt whether it ever existed, and that all we are dealing with is a myth repeated by many writers.

This is a view expanded upon by the eminent Historiographer Royal, Christopher Smout:[5]

> Let us begin with the Great Wood of Caledon. It is, in every sense of the word, a myth.

Chapter 2 has explained how there certainly was more woodland in the Highlands thousands of years ago, but that it has declined over the millennia leaving only the isolated fragments we have today. Hence Ptolemy, who received all his information second-hand, may well be applying a report of a forest, such as the fragment in Strathspey, as applicable to the whole country. In fact, the argument for 'restoring the Great Wood of Caledon' is full of holes: if 'restoration' is in fact an aim, it would be more honest to admit it is about is putting back a forest lost thousands of years ago through natural causes and that doing so goes against the natural ecological trends towards open hill; in other words, it is damaging the area's biodiversity. Having said that, there are likely to be some areas where humans were responsible for woodland loss, although this would need to be confirmed by detailed research; additionally there may be locations where humans merely accelerated a natural decline, the outcome being the same either way. In which case, is restoration sensible?

Perhaps the main origin of the anthropogenic woodland destruction myth originated with Frank Fraser Darling in the 1950s, the ecologist who originally argued that the Highlands were a devastated countryside, although it is worth noting that some of his contemporaries disagreed with him. One such was G.K. Fraser (no link with Fraser Darling), who argued that open moor could be the main natural vegetation.[6] Fraser Darling's reasoning was based on his observation that woodland was isolated in the Highlands, that its regeneration was being prevented by burning and by too many deer and sheep, and that deer numbers themselves were increasing. His belief was that woodland should be the main vegetation of the Highlands.

The belief that trees should be the plants that dominate the landscape underpins the whole reforesting movement. But, as discussed in the previous chapter, there is still little evidence that woodlands should be the main vegetation across the Highlands; indeed the presence of red deer makes it implausible in the current oligocratic phase.

Associated with the concept of woodland restoration is that of creating woodland networks. The isolated woodlands in the Highlands, so the argument goes, need joining up to create a network of woods across the land, for example across the Cairngorms from Speyside to Deeside, which is being instigated by the Cairngorms Connect project.[7] This will enable woodland plants and animals to move around, reducing the risk of extinction in isolated fragments, and benefit the biodiversity of the area generally. These linkages are often referred to as 'habitat networks', but this indicates a single-minded focus on trees,

Native pine and birch woodland in Glen Feshie, with regeneration of young trees in the foreground enabled by a major cull of red deer and resulting in unnaturally low levels of grazing. This is a common image of what the Highlands 'should' be like.

as if people are oblivious to the truism that the Highlands have the best existing network of open-ground moorland in the whole of Europe. You cannot have it both ways: any new network of trees will destroy the existing network of moorland. The point that is missed is that this existing moorland network is much more authentic than any human-made network of trees created without any historical underpinning. Currently, through isolation, each woodland fragment is different and has its own history and species. This heterogeneity is likely to become more uniform if all are joined, and it could increase the ease with which unwanted non-native species colonise.

This is not to say that the concept of creating woodland networks is wrong, just that the concept has to be applied in the right place. In lowland areas where most natural areas have disappeared because of intensive land use, joining up the existing fragments makes eminent sense. But there, fragmentation has been caused by people and is not a natural characteristic. This highlights the dominance of southern perspectives – how approaches valid in the south are applied unthinkingly to the northern fastnesses.

A view of Strathspey. As new woodlands increasingly join up to create woodland networks, the existing moorland networks fragment; the moorland is then at risk of disappearing under trees due to the inexorable rain of tree seeds.

Restoring montane scrub

Similar to the loss of woodland through human destruction, the hills once had a natural, altitudinally determined treeline, with trees being replaced by scrub at the highest levels (montane scrub). Restoring this scrub contributes to the 'ecological restoration' of the Highlands.

Anyone who walks the Scottish hills enjoys their accessibility, the ability to walk to their tops without being hindered by a barrier of trees and shrubs. In other parts of the world, mountaineers as they ascend have first to pass through woodland, followed by scrub, before the open alpine meadows are reached below the summit itself; or further north the boreal forest first fades into low scrub before the open tundra stretches out into the distance. In ecological terminology the shrubs encountered at the treeline are 'sub-alpine scrub', the alpine zone itself being above any trees, or 'sub-arctic scrub', the arctic zone being defined as beyond the province of trees.

Why is such scrub absent in Scotland? On close inspection many of the shrubs involved, such as dwarf birch, mountain willow and downy willow, do occur, but on relatively inaccessible cliffs and slopes.

The argument is that both a treeline and the associated scrub should be there but that centuries of overgrazing by sheep or deer have eaten it all so it can only survive in places grazing animals do not reach. However, it is worth quoting one of the first English tourists to the Highlands, Taylor the Water Poet, who in 1618 ascended Mount Keen in the eastern Cairngorms, perhaps one of the first recorded ascents of a Munro.[8]

> The next day I travelled over an exceeding high mountain, called mount Skeene [Mt Keen], where I found the valley very warme before I went up it ; but when I came to the top of it, my teeth beganne to dance in my head with cold, like virginals jacks ; and withall, a most familiar mist embraced me round, that I could not see thrice my length any way : withall, it yielded so friendly a deaw, that it did moisten thorow my clothes ; where the old proverb of a Scottish miste was verified, in wetting me to the skinne. Up and downe, I think this hill is six miles, the way so uneven, stony, and full of bogges, quagmires, and long heath, that a dogge with three legs will out-runne a horse with four .

Note that Taylor does not report having to pass through any trees or shrubs on the way to the top, only long heather and peat bogs. Similarly, 150 years later in 1771, the naturalist James Robertson noted when travelling through the eastern Cairngorms:[9]

> In my progress thro' these mountains I saw no trees growing.

Peat, especially blanket peat, is common in the Highlands on hill tops, especially on rounded hills; if its profile is studied, except at lower altitudes, woody remains of trees and shrubs are absent. In other words, scrub must have been absent at the time peat-forming plants colonised the landscape. This confirms the eminent ecologist Duncan Poore's conclusion in 1997 that:[10]

> There is little evidence that there was extensive scrub on the mountains within the current climatic period.

In other words it must have been centuries or millennia since it was present, if it ever was, which certainly rules out sheep as causing its demise; it only became possible to keep sheep in any number in the Highland landscape once the wolf had been made extinct around 1700. In the Southern Uplands of Scotland sheep farming was possible from an earlier period because wolves had already been eradicated.

The absence of high-level scrub and trees in the Highlands is due to poor soils and the natural presence of grazing animals. Alpine and arctic regions are characterised by consistent winter snow cover, snow that protects the trees from browsing and so allows the scrub to survive. But the Highlands have a 'montane' climate – a lot of rain and neither heat in summer nor particular cold in winter. There is not consistent year-to-year snow cover, and grazing animals, especially red deer, can wander up and down the hill at will and mountain hares can eat any shrubs all year round. In winter, when there is nothing else to eat, the buds of the willow shrubs are particularly palatable and a joy to eat: the willows have no chance of taking over, and so are restricted to the inaccessible places, particularly those localised ones that geologically result in better soils. The shrubs present are remnants from immediate postglacial times, when the climate really was arctic and there was plentiful snow to protect it: they represent relict sub-arctic scrub.

The one location in the Highlands with an altitudinal treeline, Coire Buidhe above Inshriach in Strathspey. Just because such a treeline exists in one place does not mean there should be such a treeline across the Highlands.

Willow scrub developing at 750 metres, below Meall nan Tarmachan in Perthshire. The willows, a relict postglacial population, hung on here because of the area's calcium-rich soils. They are now expanding within a deer- and sheep-proof enclosure. It is hard to see how such expansion will continue if the fence is taken down.

This scrub may have been able to expand somewhat during colder epochs with more snow, such as during the Little Ice Age,[11] but is basically on the way out, albeit clinging on in a few places.

It is possible, therefore, that there is no such thing as montane scrub, at least in countries where grazing animals are naturally present: it is merely a theoretical idea hard to conceptualise in practice. Yet nowadays there are many projects trying to create this habitat, by building fenced enclosures to exclude grazing, by growing on and planting out shrubs in these areas, or by trying to reduce grazing in the wider landscape to a level at which the shrubs can survive, a level way below any natural one. It is hard to see any long-term benefit from this, for when the fences come down the animals will pour back in, and grazing reduction in the wider landscape is hard to achieve in the long term.

The whole 'montane scrub restoration' bandwagon, for conservation action is as subject to current fashions as any other discipline, is another example of not realising the distinctiveness or even uniqueness of the Highland landscape, or understanding its long-term ecological history. It is seeing something elsewhere in the world, in this case abundant scrub, and assuming it should also be here. It also illustrates that some ecological concepts are so strong in the imagination that they are perceived as self-evident truths – for example that all mountains have treelines and that trees should be the top plant everywhere in Scotland. Many mountains in other parts of the world have a treeline but it does not follow that all mountains must have one. A distinctive feature of the Highland landscape at the global level is that treelines are absent owing to its montane climate.

The need to restore riparian woodland

The rivers of the Highlands often have their banks bare of trees owing to the presence of too many grazing animals, which prevent the trees' regeneration. Planting riverside trees (riparian woodland) not only contributes to 'ecological restoration' but also increases the productivity of the rivers for fish and pearl mussels.

The banks of most rivers meandering through the glens are bare, or at least trees are few and far between. Riverbanks with their flood-deposited alluvium provide nutrient-rich grasslands and therefore some of the best grazing in an otherwise infertile landscape. Deer are drawn in and so are in direct competition with any trees trying to colonise the area: is it fair to the deer to remove some of their best grazing by planting trees? The deer themselves do not stop to think that riversides should be avoided because everyone knows that trees are good things for rivers, stabilising the banks, shading the water from the summer heat, dropping leaves into the water as the first link in the food chain, benefiting salmon and pearl mussels into the bargain. No, the deer concentrate on their own needs first.

However for the benefits just outlined riverbanks are singled out for woodland creation, an approach that illustrates how we compartmentalise the Highland landscape in both our minds and reality. We first break it up into its separate components – riverbanks, woods, grassland, heathland, peat bogs – and try to manage each independently of the others, for they often have incompatible needs: we cannot expand

Small blocks of trees planted along the banks of Clunie Water in the glen leading to Braemar. This is to create riparian woodland to help shade the river in summer and provide leaf litter to benefit freshwater invertebrates and in turn salmon. This illustrates a compartmentalised view of the landscape.

woodland, for example, without reducing something else – heathland or grass perhaps. We fence them all off individually and then decide how many deer, cattle or hares will be allowed in each, if any at all. This may be necessary if all we have are isolated patches of nature in an intensively farmed lowland landscape, but in the free-ranging Scottish uplands it makes no sense at all. It misses the wider picture of the integrated whole, that nature has no predetermined plan of what should be where, of maximising everything (a human wish) or of keeping everything in 'favourable condition', an impossible task.[12] It does not allow for different habitats fluctuating under varying natural pressures, often with a hint of randomness thrown in, such as a localised flash flood, a landslide or the chance colonisation of a particular species.

But back to riversides. Akin to the absence of montane scrub, the absence of riverside trees is most likely a natural characteristic of many Highland rivers and burns. If we want to keep a wild Highland landscape we just have to accept that our rivers may not be as productive as they could be. Because salmon is a declining species there is a strong imperative to manage for it, but this should not be at the expense of the wild landscape; in any case, most of the problems causing the decline of salmon appear to be at sea, where conservation effort should be concentrated. The landscape has had treeless rivers for thousands of years. What has suddenly changed?

This also raises the question of whether we should be managing the land for individual plants or animals perceived to be at risk, or for the landscape as a whole. There is a strong tendency for each interest group to identify the rarest species of the type they like, whether moss, bird or beetle, and argue that we should manage for that. Bearing in mind the number of species present in the Highland landscape, it is impossible to manage them all individually and it becomes arbitrary to select any particular species, whether rare or common. But we have an affinity for rarity, ascribing greater value to rare things, so much action today is about trying to make rare species common, often without considering the wider ecological picture of why they are rare in the first place. As an example, aspen is a rare tree in the Highlands and there is a strong push to make it more common. But surely, if naturally rare, there is no case for increasing its abundance?

Natural ecosystems come and go and we should not worry too much if we lose plants or animals, particularly those at the edge of their range and so more likely to become extinct if conditions change. Indeed, regarding lowland heathlands, Clive Chatters warns against micro-managing for individual species rather than the wider whole.[13] This whole micro-management approach is caused by compartmentalised thinking, which is anathema to the conservation of ecosystems at the landscape scale appropriate to the Highlands. If new species naturally come in, fine, if some disappear, also fine: surely this is what it means to let nature be wild. There is a strong tendency to blame anything we do not like on us humans: if something becomes extinct, it must be our fault, so something must be done. But our interference is preventing us from fully understanding nature.

Preventing overgrazing

The Highlands are treeless because humans have introduced too many grazing animals (sheep) or allowed the population of native herbivores (red deer) to expand above any natural level. The result is an overgrazed landscape of damaged habitats.

We often hear about overgrazing by sheep or deer. But how do we know there are too many deer? Because there are too few trees. How do we know there are too few trees? Because there are too many deer, of course. A win-win argument if ever there was one!

This concept is accepted without thinking through the expected impact of grazing animals on natural ecosystems. Its dubiety was discussed in Chapter 2, yet the literature of conservation organisations is littered with it. Particularly common in the popular press is the idea that sheep farming has been responsible for significant woodland loss in the Highlands, an idea so easy to refute that one wonders why it is still current. It was only possible to introduce extensive sheep grazing in the Highlands after the wolf was made extinct, and before the Battle of Culloden the wealth of the Highlander was measured in cattle not sheep; any sheep present were likely to have been small in number and wintered indoors. Only after Culloden, with the introduction of modern landowning,

Sheep farming has an undeservedly bad press. The vast majority of woods in the Highlands disappeared centuries before the advent of commercial sheep farming.

did sheep farming take off on a large scale, associated in many places with the expulsion of the local population – the notorious Highland Clearances. But to paraphrase Tom Devine,[14] when people contemplate hills and glens that have no people they should not assume people were there in the past.

A glance at the Roy Maps of 1747–52 indicates low coverage of woodland in the Highlands.[15] Most woodlands shown then are still present today: the woods disappeared way before the sheep farming was introduced. Generally, livestock grazing in the hills has always been low owing to the difficulty of maintaining animals through the winter, as noted by James Robertson when visiting the northern Cairngorms in 1771:[16]

> The small spots of arable land which are found in the valleys alone, bear a small proportion to the hilly & cultivated parts, on which the people depend for pasture. Cattle being the chief objection of attention, a man who pays £3 sterling of annual rent will perhaps have 20 black Cattle, 3 or 4 Horses, 20 Sheep & 10 Goats. During the summer or & autumn the pastures could maintain thrice that number, but they would perish during the winter or spring. Even the scanty, stock to which the Farmer confines himself is with difficulty preserved & not unfrequently some of them die for want of fodder.

During the sheep farming era that followed the Highland Clearances, although the total number of sheep was high, grazing levels were not because the sheep ranged over such large areas. For example, King and Nicholson state that in 1952 the densities of free-ranging sheep on upland farms ranged from around 25 per square kilometre in the far north to 167 in the south of the area, with most areas having a density of 50 to 100 per square kilometre.[17] One hundred may sound a large number, but if spread over a square kilometre it equates to one sheep in each hectare (two and a half acres) – in practice a very low grazing level in British agricultural terms. In the north each sheep would have four hectares (ten acres) to graze. There may have been some localised loss or thinning out of woods caused by the sheep, but at a strategic level there is no way sheep deserve the bad reputation they have in many quarters. Indeed, an observant ecologist can even see in some locations the expansion of native birch woodland in the presence of significant numbers of sheep.[18]

Although the native red deer and sheep have similar grazing preferences, it is the deer which has been the greater influence in keeping woodland in check. It is certainly true that deer numbers have been increasing across Scotland in recent years, but at the same time sheep numbers have been declining in tandem with the decline of sheep farming. Sheep and deer do not like to share the same pastures so to some extent there is mutual exclusion. Therefore, it is not surprising that deer numbers rise as sheep numbers fall, which explains some, but not necessarily all, of the current increase.

Presumably deer numbers fell to make way for the sheep from the late 1700s onwards, although it is very difficult to get an estimation of the numbers of deer in the landscape before then. The observations of the aforementioned Taylor the Water Poet who witnessed

Red deer in Lairig Gartain, Glencoe.

a deer hunt in 1618 in the Royal Forest of Mar, west of Braemar, make for interesting reading, not only about deer hunting but for his general observations of the area:[19]

> I saw the ruins of an old castle, called the castle of Kindroghit [in current Braemar] ... it was the last house I saw in those parts: for I was the space of twelve days after, before I saw either house, corne-field, or habitation for any creature, but deere, wilde horses, wolves, and such like creatures ... the first day we traveled eight miles, where there were built small cottages built on purpose to lodge in, which they call Lonquhards...

> [M]any kettles and pots boyling ... venison, bak't, sodden, rost, and steu'de, beefe, mutton, goates, kid, hares, fresh salmon, pidgeons, hens, capons, chickens, partridge, moorecoots, heathcocks, caperkellies, and tarmagants [ptarmigan]; good ale, sacke, white, and claret, tent or allegant [tinto, Alicante], with most potent Aquavitæ.

> [O]ur campe, which consisteth of foureteen or fifteene hundred men and horses; the manner of hunting is this : Five or six hundred men do rise early in the morning, and they doe disperse themselves divers ways, and seven, eight, or tenne miles compasse, thcy doe bring chase to the deere in many heards (two, three, or foure hundred in a heard) to such or such a place, as the noblemen shall appoint them ... Then after we had stayed there three houres or thereabouts, we might perceive the deere apperare on the hills round about us ... in a space of two houres fourscore fat deere were slaine ...

Taylor demonstrates that there were a lot of red deer in the Cairngorms in 1618, and this may have been so in other parts of the Highlands although this is hard to determine. Later, the botanist James Robertson who toured the Highlands from 1767 to 1771 observed that there were numerous herds of red and roe deer in the Cairngorms.[20] Donald Monro, who visited the Hebrides in 1549, talked of "many deer" on the islands of Mull, Skye and Raasay, of Jura being "a fine forrest for deer" and of there being "abundant little deer" on the island of Rum.[21] Martin Martin, who visited around 1695, talked of "some hundred of deer in the mountain" of Rum.[22] On Skye James Robertson noted in 1771:[23]

> There are a good number of Deer which are frequently troublesom to the Farmers often making inroads into the Corn when it begins to ripen and to prevent the destruction they generally make They are obliged to watch the Corn during the night to ward off these animals.

It is possible to speculate that during the Jacobite uprisings those forced to flee into the hills killed many deer in order to survive, thus over time reducing their numbers.

The issue can be tackled from a theoretical viewpoint. The maximum number of grazing animals in a locality is dependent on the amount of food available in winter (or in other parts of the world in the dry season). If the rate of plant growth is known, the number of animals it will feed can be calculated. Such a calculation for the Highlands indicates that there should be significantly more animals than the low numbers necessary fo trees to survive;[24] this is the ultimate reason why the Highland landscape is largely treeless.

Additionally, recent research suggests that across Europe as a whole there are far fewer grazing animals than would be expected in natural ecosystems – because humans have seriously depleted their numbers or made them extinct.[25] The recent book *Rewilding* concludes that "advances in ecological science have firmly positioned herbivores at the core of processes that produce vibrant ecosystems." [26] This means that the Highland landscape, having retained significant populations of red deer throughout the postglacial period, must be more natural than most others in Europe, perhaps the most natural? There is nothing natural about low grazing levels, which is why regeneration of trees brought about by the elimination of, or a major reduction in, grazing can in no way be called *natural* regeneration; it is more *forced* regeneration. If trees have no protection from browsing, whether winter snow, thorny shrubs, inaccessibility, or abundant regeneration and growth from optimum conditions, the landscape is likely to be open.[27] Surely this is the simplest explanation and, applying Occam's Razor, are not the simplest explanations the best?

The Highlands, though, cannot be seen as being comprised of completely natural ecosystems because apex predators – the top carnivores – are missing, in particular the wolf. The forests disappeared when wolves were present, so even if wolves were brought back, there is 10,000 years of evidence to show that they would not reduce deer numbers enough to cause a resurgence in woodland cover. Indeed, there is still debate as to whether the presence of wolves significantly reduces deer populations at all.[28]

There is also a generic claim bandied about that grazing animals cause 'habitat damage' and that this is a bad thing: they eat trees, damage heather, restrict interesting plants to inaccessible cliffs, trample peat bogs …. But isn't this what happens in natural ecosystems? An animal cannot survive without eating and trampling (damaging) something. It is worth noting that red deer have recently been introduced to a lowland heath in England to increase the diversity of habitats and species present.[29]

Another point often missed is that grazing animals maintain the fertility of ecosystems through their urine and dung, these being plant nutrients: think of the manure we shovel onto our garden to keep things going. It is the same in natural systems: without animals to recycle them, nutrients remain locked up in organic matter. Hence, removing animals is likely to reduce the fertility of the whole landscape. Finally, the anthropogenic reduction of herbivores appears also to increase the fire risk in ecosystems because the animals prevent the accumulation of inflammable dead plant material.[30]

Large numbers of animals may well cause a problem to us humans, whether raiding our fields and gardens or being things we crash into as we drive along our roads, but this is a different issue. Large animals are 'a problem' across the world when they want to share space with us. But a landscape or world without them is a sterile place.

Reversing the damage from the industrial exploitation of native woods
Contributing to the loss of the Great Wood of Caledon was exploitation to provide timber, charcoal for iron smelting and bark for leather tanning.

Along with sheep and deer, the loss of Highland woods has commonly been ascribed to felling and timber extraction. Localised felling has most likely been occurring since the first human inhabitants, but Richard Tipping has told us that the trees generally regenerated in these clearings: cleared forest provides an excellent seedbed for young trees.[31] Owing to the usefulness of wood it is also likely that native woodlands would in many places have been looked after and managed by native people: it was in their interests to do so.

Taylor the Water Poet, after evocatively describing the deer hunt at Mar in the eastern Cairngorms, continues:[32]

> [A]nd after supper, a fire of firre-wood as high as an indifferent may-pole : for I assure you, that the Earle of Marr will give any man that is his friend, for thankes, as many firre-trees (that are as good as any shippes masts in England) as are worth (if they were in any place neere the Thames, or any other portable river) the best Earldome in England or Scotland either : For I dare affirme, hee hath as many growing there, as would serve for masts (from this time to the end of the worlde) for all the shippes, carackes, hoyes, galleys, boats, drumlers, barkes, and water-crafts, that are now, or can be in this world these fourty yeeres. … they doe grow so farre away from any passage of water, and withal in such rockie mountains, that no way to convey them is possible to be passable, either with boate, horse, or cart.

These pine woods are presumably the same woods illustrated by Farquharson in his estate map of 1703[33] and later mapped by General Roy, and are the forebears of the current native pinewoods at Mar Lodge. There appears to have been little significant change in woodland cover since 1618, although there has certainly been both thinning within the

The old Bonawe iron furnace on the shores of Loch Etive in Argyll.

woods and planting since then. It is also interesting to note from the Farquharson map that there were no outlying pinewoods in 1703, indicating that most of the area was open moorland even then, any woodland decline to the current area being an ancient event.[34]

Taylor's observations show that these pinewoods were of no economic value because there was no way of extracting the timber as the Highlands had no roads then. This makes commercial timber extraction an unlikely cause of forest loss in the region other than in Strathspey, and to a lesser extent in Deeside and around Loch Ness. But, as discussed earlier, in these locations the situation is complicated: it is difficult to untangle the extent to which humans managed the forest for their own ends, preventing natural decline in the process, from the extent to which humans destroyed the forest.

The first commercial ironworks in the Highlands was probably that of Sir George Hay dating from 1610 at Loch Maree in Wester Ross, owing to the presence of woodland in the area and its good access to the sea. It should be remembered that woodland was always localised here, the main vegetation for the past 4,000 years having been open moorland.[35]

In the early days peat charcoal was used for iron smelting in addition to wood charcoal, so the industry is likely to have affected both the woodland and the peat bogs. However, the woods are still there, suggesting that the iron smelting did not result in their destruction, although it is impossible to determine the extent to which the industry reduced the total woodland cover. In any case, if the woods were felled we would expect them to have naturally regenerated: the northern slopes above the Loch Maree fault provide optimum conditions for woodland, which is why it was there in the first place.

For ironworks further south Lindsay concludes:[36]

The largest and longest-lived of the [ironworks], the Bonawe Furnace in Argyll, needed 10,000 acres of oak coppice to keep going, and left the woods in at least as extensive condition when it closed in 1876 as when it opened in 1753.

Christopher Smout adds:[37]

The same could be said of the much more widespread users of oak coppice, the tanbarkers, who operated throughout Argyll, Perthshire, Dunbartonshire, and Stirlingshire.

It was in the interests of those exploiting the woods not to destroy them but to manage them, and even to extend woodland cover. It is certainly true that felling of native pinewoods during both world wars thinned out many of them, perhaps causing a reduction in extent in some locations. But if the conditions were right for woodland to exist in the first place, the felled areas would be expected to regenerate. The fundamental point is that when this exploitation started trees were already rare in the landscape for reasons other than exploitation: from a strategic Highland-wide perspective, the modification or loss of a habitat that is already rare makes little difference in the grand order of things.

The restoration of peat bogs

Eroding peatlands are common across the Highlands, the erosion largely originating from poor land management. Hence, most peatlands are in need of 'restoration' which, as well as restoring them to their natural state, will also prevent the release of their stored carbon. Additionally, humans have dug ditches across peatland and planted trees on it, actions that also result in the loss of its stored carbon – to the detriment of the climate.

'Everyone' seems to know that erosion is a bad thing and needs to be arrested; everyone knows that peat bogs are eroding – think of the endless peat haggs – and because humans are generally antithetical to nature, the cause of the erosion must be us humans. Therefore it must be stopped! This illustrates a lack of understanding of the long-term, millennial-scale dynamics of bogs: they grow, they naturally erode, they grow again.[38]

'Restoring' such erosion, like trying to regenerate woodland, is going against nature and making the landscape less wild, particularly if diggers are taken onto the hill to block ditches, create dams and re-profile the haggs. There is a dilemma here, though: preventing peat erosion may reduce the amount of peat releasing carbon back into the air, thereby

A natural gully in a high-altitude blanket peat in the Monadhliath Mountains. Note the tree stumps at the bottom of the peat, which show that this area was wooded thousands of years ago. Such erosion is a natural feature of peatlands. Revegetating the exposed peat to reduce carbon loss reduces the naturalness of peatland ecosystems – probably with only limited climate benefit.

A network of ditches (moor grips) in blanket peat. Unlike the infilling of natural gullies, blocking these will help restore the peatland to its natural state.

achieving a small amount of global warming mitigation. So which is more important: biodiversity conservation, which means no intervention, allowing natural processes to dominate – especially because Scotland is a world centre for blanket peat – or intervening on behalf of the climate, which inevitably results in us continuing to take over the planet?

There is a lot of talk of peat bogs having to play their part in stopping global warming by managing them to store more carbon, 'rewetting' being a phrase commonly used. But our expectations of them are too high. Many of the peatlands across the Highlands are ancient, nearing the end of their natural lives: they have lost the will to create more peat, instead taking the phoenix route.[39] They will still remain an important store of carbon but they have lost the ability to increase this store: they are not a silver bullet to save us from ourselves.

Thus, surely, in a world centre of peatlands, we should let them be. I am referring to *natural* erosion of bogs. Most erosion in the Scottish uplands is natural but not all. Many of the blanket peatlands in England at the southern end of the Pennines have been damaged, but this is much less the case in Scotland – although even here drainage ditches can be seen dug through even remote areas of bog, a practice at one time grant-aided by the government. Where bogs have been damaged by human activity there certainly is a strong case for restoration to their natural state, by filling these drains, removing forest plantations or revegetating the bog surface.

But if red deer trample peatland, causing erosion, 'twas ever thus. We must resist the temptation to intervene just because we see something we do not like. If we are restoring undamaged peatland for the sake of the climate, we might be damaging an internationally important type of landscape. Such restoration could leave no part of the Highlands untouched by the hand of humans. If we are serious about climate change in relation to peatlands, the best thing do, as discussed later, is to stop further tree planting on shallow peats and peaty soils: the trees oxidise the soil carbon and prevent the bogs becoming long-term carbon stores as the peat slowly deepens over time.

The provision of ecosystem services
Natural ecosystems provide many services that benefit humans, and should be conserved or restored for this reason.

This approach relates to the modern concepts of 'ecosystem services', 'nature-based solutions' and 'natural capital', which are based on the need to protect ecosystems for the benefits they provide to us, and on the fact that nature can solve some of our problems: working with nature is better than working against it. The aim here is not to provide a critique of the concepts, which are important, but to illustrate the fact that the Highland landscape is not very good at many of these things, with the exception of the role of shallow peats in acting as long-term carbon sinks. Certainly the landscape provides Scotland with water, an essential service, but this water can also be detrimental to us if there is too much – it causes floods. Floods may benefit natural ecosystems by bringing nutrients down from the hills to provide fertile flood plains, but they are anathema to us humans.

Conservation organisations claim that adding trees to the Highland landscape will result in multiple ecosystem services or, in plain English, multiple benefits: trees prevent flooding and erosion, they benefit the climate by storing carbon, they are good for biodiversity, they are good for the economy, they are good for recreation and for the landscape generally. These are easy things to trot out but all are debatable. Below is a brief summary of each. If the benefits are questionable, should we be so cavalier in reshaping the pattern of the Highland landscape?

Preventing flooding and erosion
The unwooded hills of the Highlands contribute to downstream flooding, which would be remedied if the rate of water run-off was reduced through the presence of trees. Additionally, restoring damaged peatlands, so that they retain more water, will reduce the flood risk.

Although a lot of water is stored in blanket peat it does not flow in or out, being held in place by capillary action. Hence such ecosystems are not good at flood control.

The presence of trees certainly can slow the rate of water run-off into rivers, but most flood damage is caused during extreme rainfall or snow-melt events when the presence of trees makes little difference. On arid tropical soils the presence of trees slows soil erosion, but there is little evidence that this will also be the case on Scottish hill slopes with tightly bound vegetation; indeed, after extreme rainfall events erosion gullies can be seen in both wooded and unwooded locations, particularly along watercourses. An example is the landslides through the forested slopes above the east shores of Loch Lomond in the 1980s.

Contrary to popular belief, landscapes of blanket peat are not very good at flood control because water cannot drain into or out of the peat; only the surface layer of the peat absorbs rain. Neither are peatlands very good at providing good-quality water: water from such landscapes is anathema to water treatment companies because it is difficult to purify for human use: its colour prevents sterilisation by ultra violet, and its high concentration of acids prevents sterilisation by chlorine due to the production of toxic trihalomethanes. Sometimes it also has a high concentrations of aluminium.

Trees are good for the climate
Forests store a lot of carbon in their wood. Therefore increasing the forest cover will mitigate global warming by removing carbon from the air.

There are four ways in which the presence of forests can affect the climate, two related to their role in carbon storage and two to their direct effect on temperature.

Dark, three-dimensional trees absorb more solar radiation than lighter coloured two-dimensional moorland, resulting in localised warming. More research is needed on this topic.

In terms of carbon storage, trees take carbon dioxide out of the air through photosynthesis and store the collected carbon in their trunks, branches, leaves and roots. Hence, as a newly created forest grows and builds up its biomass, it can contribute directly to global warming mitigation. But when fully mature or felled, when trees die and are replaced by young trees, the forest will have reached a steady state and, while still a large store of carbon, will no longer be taking more carbon out of the air than it returns through respiration and decomposition. In other words, trees cannot go on taking carbon out of the air for ever.

The second part they can play has the opposite effect, adding stored carbon to the air and being detrimental to global warming mitigation. This is when trees are planted on peat or peaty soil: here their roots extract water and dry out the soil, causing the stored organic matter to decay and oxidise back into the air. Indeed, it is now government policy not to plant trees on deep peat for this very reason and it is why commercial plantations which were planted on peat bogs, such as those in Caithness and Sutherland, are being removed. However, calculations show that only about a 12cm depth of humus or peat will store as much carbon as a commercial Sitka spruce forest,[40] so it makes equal sense not to plant trees on shallow peat; after all, a tree does not know whether it has been planted on deep or shallow peat!

In terms of their direct effect on temperature, again there are two contradictory mechanisms. Treelines are moving north over open tundra in northern Canada so that in winter two-dimensional reflective snow is being replaced by dark, three-dimensional trees that absorb the sun's heat. This reduction in reflectivity, or 'albedo' results in localised warming. The same effect is likely to occur in the Highlands when trees are planted on the paler moorland, reducing the albedo of the landscape.

But trees can also have the opposite effect, particularly in the tropics, by cooling the climate through evaporation of water from their leaves.

In summary, it is simplistic to argue that planting trees will benefit the climate, particularly in the Highlands where most soils are rich in carbon: here, the trees' role in both releasing soil carbon and reducing landscape reflectivity, may well mean that the trees will have the opposite effect to that intended – making global warming worse. In contrast, planting trees on lowland soils with a low carbon content may well be beneficial to the climate.

In spite of this, many trees are being planted on carbon-rich soils, including shallow peats, when, from a global warming perspective, it would be best to let these areas develop over hundreds of years into full-grown peat bogs, storing a lot more carbon as the peat builds up than would any forest. Shallow peats have a much longer life ahead of them than the older, deeper peats, which are more likely to stop storing carbon and erode away. But the locations most commonly planted in the Highlands today are the gentler slopes at the bases of hills – the locations with the best long-term storage of carbon through peat development. It is not sensible to do this if global warming is being taken seriously.

Tree roots extract water, causing soil carbon to oxidise in drier conditions and leading to the release of carbon into the air. Planting on peaty soils may not benefit the climate.

Additionally, the way in which the trees are planted, whether by ploughing or mounding, also releases the carbon stored in the soil, as does the industrial process of felling and harvesting at the end of the forest rotation by churning up the soil.

There needs to be more discrimination as to where trees are planted. The Highlands are not a good place to use trees to solve our climate problems and the recent large-scale tree planting schemes in the name of carbon offsetting are a cause for concern.

Trees are good for biodiversity
Adding trees to the landscape is good for Highland biodiversity.

Following the definition given in Chapter 2, 'biodiversity' is used here to mean 'the natural ecological characteristics of the Highlands' – the number and arrangement of plants and animals provided by nature. Woodland is certainly a natural characteristic of the Highlands and does contribute to the area's biodiversity. Some woods hold internationally important populations of rare mosses, liverworts and lichens, although others are not particularly species rich. The extent of native woodland peaked in the mesocratic phase and most woods have been naturally declining ever since, or at last have remained static in extent.

But there is all the difference between these ancient woods with an unbroken ecological link back to the end of the Ice Age, and new woods of native trees planted on land that has been naturally treeless for hundreds or thousands of years. Such planting will damage the biodiversity of the Highlands, reducing its naturalness. For example, it is sad to see how the landscape integrity around the relict Glas Leitire pinewood at Kinlochewe in Wester Ross has been damaged by all the action to extend the wood southwards through planting and fencing; the area is now a map showing the different approaches to woodland expansion undertaken here over the years. The vegetation pattern of this area has been static for 4,000 years, albeit with some tree felling in the past, so the pattern was relatively natural before all the tree expansion action of the past few decades: the area is now a landscape muddle and the original ecological integrity has been lost.

If you plant trees on part of an open moorland the diversity of the area will increase because it will host plants and animals characteristic of both woodland and moorland rather than in just one of them alone. But 'diversity' in this sense is not the same as 'biodiversity' as here defined. One habitat can only be created at the expense of another, so new woodland of a common European type created at the expense of globally rare moorland will reduce the extent of internationally important open-ground habitats, reducing overall global biodiversity.

Additionally, there are over-high expectations of the nature conservation value of the new native-tree woodlands. When thinking of Scots pine forest, people probably hold in their imagination beautiful, large-crowned, widely spaced trees, which are an asset to any landscape. But many of the new trees have been planted close together (to receive

Scots pine trees colonising heather moorland at Glen Feshie following a major cull of deer. The species characteristic of pinewoods are different from those of open moorland. If the natural biodiversity characteristic of the landscape is open moorland, then global biodiversity will be lost if the area is converted to pine wood.

tree-planting grants from the government), and many will grow tall, straight and spindly, some dying early, many blowing over. This is especially the case for woods planted without ground preparation by forest ploughing, which helps the trees but destroys the landscape. Many of these new plantations reflect the lack of understanding of the ecology of the Highlands by those planting the trees. Additionally, particularly in the west of Scotland, many of the trees have been planted on flower-rich wet heathland containing plants such as milkwort, lousewort, cross-leaved heath, heath-spotted orchid and bog asphodel, all low-growing, if restrained, summer colour. Once the tree canopy closes, these species will be shaded out, resulting in a monotonous understorey dominated by purple moor grass (see bottom picture of p. 133). It is hard to see the conservation benefit of these new woods.

If these woods are eventually exploited for their timber, massive roads will be bulldozed into the hills to enable access for the massive machinery which is part and parcel of timber harvesting. If not exploited, they will be left to blow over. What space is left for wildness?

Stopping damaging management of moorland for grouse

Heather moorland is intensively managed for red grouse and is bad for biodiversity and the climate.

Shooting grouse in places where the moors are not managed is a relatively benign land use, being the sustainable harvest of a natural crop, but it is certainly true that the management of the heather moors that characterises the eastern side of the Highlands has become intensive in many places. The issue of intensive grouse moor management is now highly politicised, politics which I have no desire to enter into here. It is also true that killing species seen as antithetical to the shooting interests ('vermin') has resulted in fewer animals in the landscapes and the extinction of some such as the polecat. However,

The moorland of the eastern Highlands is an ancient landscape.

in keeping with the focus of this book, only the landscape impacts are considered here. The two main ones are the burning of the heather to benefit the grouse, which creates a mosaic of burnt and unburnt heather across the hill, and the bulldozing of tracks into the hills to make it easier to get up to the moors; this latter issue is discussed later (p. 112). There are also minor landscape impacts such as the construction of grouse butts, the digging of small pools and the spreading of grit.

Burning heather to benefit red grouse may well provide a greater variety of habitats for plants, insects and breeding waders. If carried out with respect to the weather and time of year, in particular when the soil is still wet, it need not permanently damage the soils or plants, including those growing on blanket peat, because most of these plants are dormant in winter and new shoots will grow up from below. Where it is dry heather moor being burnt, the practice will have little impact on the climate, for it is not releasing fossil carbon but merely recycling carbon which would otherwise be released from the soil as the plant material naturally decays.

The situation is different on blanket peat where burning will reduce the rate at which peat forms: although the peat itself is not damaged, the plant material burnt off would otherwise become incorporated into peat sequestering carbon, to the benefit of the climate. However, recent research suggests that this may be counteracted to some extent by the creation of charcoal, which has a high carbon content and is very resistant to decay, eventually becoming incorporated into the peat.[41]

A difficulty, though, is that on level or gently sloping ground it can be very difficult to know whether the vegetation is peat-forming or not: peat bogs do not start as peat. Deep peat starts as shallow peat and shallow peat develops from humus-rich soils. Peat will not form on steeper ground, though, so if burning is to continue, gentle slopes should be avoided. There is a case for retaining some controlled burning to prevent the occasional accidental or lightning-induced large fire, which could otherwise destroy the soil and peat; such fires are likely to be more common in the Highlands in a warming climate, a climate in which thunderstorms are still relatively rare. As humans have caused the decline of grazing animals across the world, including a strong push to reduce grazing across the Highlands, the incidence of wildfires has increased.[42] Hence, an alternative to controlled fires for the suppression of damaging uncontrolled fires is to ensure there is a significant level of grazing across the landscape.

The pattern of burning is visible from a distance. For some it adds an interesting aesthetic pattern to the Highland landscape, for others it is symbolic of an undesirable practice. What it does do is reduce the wildness of the land by imprinting the hand of man, and reduce the naturalness of the ecology, adding a diversity that would not otherwise be present. However, the desire by many to restrict grouse shooting and muirburn, and to stop or enshroud it in further regulation, may cause many landowners to give up grouse shooting altogether. The most likely alternative land use is conversion to Sitka spruce plantations because it is government policy to increase significantly the tree cover of Scotland; such plantations are of little landscape or wildlife value. An unexpected consequence of stopping muirburn is the increased likelihood of the moors being colonised by trees soon after. Naturally, heather moorland consists of dense stands of old growth that are relatively resistant to tree invasion; fires are rare and only caused by lightning. But areas frequently burnt are a good seedbed: if burning were stopped, trees could rapidly take over. This is likely because so many trees have been planted, creating plentiful seed sources, and because grazing has been so reduced that young trees can flourish.

If burning is stopped, any trees seeding into the heather will need to be removed if we want to retain these ancient landscapes, for the heather moors are not the result of landowners managing the land for grouse: they are antique landscapes, expanding naturally over the millennia as the woodland declined. Indeed, outside of the British Isles, the red grouse–heather ecosystem is found nowhere else in the world: Scotland is the world centre. They should be celebrated for contributing to the essence of the Highlands, an essence that can be found distilled in those great delicacies: heather honey and malt whisky.

Burning does not kill the vegetation if carried out when the soil is wet. By burning off the dead plant remains, it reduces the amount of carbon input to the soil. On peatland, burning reduces the rate of carbon sequestration – the amount incorporated into peat.

Burning on blanket peat may slow the rate of peat formation; on bracken it will encourage more bracken; on richer soils with grazing it will cause heather loss; on high-altitude, low-growing heath it will be unnecessary. If continued, it is best done on the steeper, drier, heather-clad slopes.

View of a wild, unsullied moorland landscape in the eastern Highlands: Beinn A' Ghlo from Glas Maol. An antique land.

Chapter 4 Understanding

Changes in the Highland landscape since the Battle of Culloden

We have seen how the Battle of Culloden in 1746 was epoch-making, not only for the changes it brought about to the culture of the Highlands but also as a turning point for the management of the physical landscape. Before Culloden, the hills and moors suffered only from benign neglect, remaining in "a state of nature" as the 18th-century naturalist James Robertson put it.[1] The exception was the area in or around human settlements, the inbye land, where the vegetation and landscape would have been heavily modified for growing crops, for cutting peats for fuel and, where trees were present, for woodland management.

This chapter illustrates the landscape changes brought about since 1746, presented in the rough chronological order they were introduced, although most of them overlap in time. Changes within the settlements themselves are not considered, only the impacts on the hills and moors beyond.

Old peat-cuttings on the island of Islay

Peat-cuttings

Peat continued to be cut into modern times because it was widely available and there was no other fuel to hand. However, with the improvement in transport links, coal from the Central Belt began to take over, first by sea and later by road and rail. The cutting of the peats was a communal activity and once it ceased the whole culture of peat-cutting, so adequately described by Sandy Fenton,[2] disappeared. However peat-cutting by hand can still be seen, although such cuttings are nowadays few and far between.

Mechanisation has taken over from manual cutting, with the peat being either sold commercially for fuel or cut for the whisky industry. Peat cut for the horticultural industry largely comes from lowland peat bogs outwith the Highlands.

Old peat-cuttings are a common part of the Highland scenery and much of the flatter land near to existing and earlier settlements consists of land which once was peat-covered. Peat growth may eventually resume, but the process takes thousands of years.

Traditional hand-cutting of peat in Wester Ross.

Peat has been removed from the foreground as far back as the vertical edge visible in the middle distance, the limit of hand-cutting of peat for fuel. Location is Naast, Wester Ross. Peat is regrowing in the cut-over areas.

Mechanised peat extraction in Caithness in the 1980s for sale as a fuel.

This landscape on Fair Isle was once peat-covered but the peat has been removed over the centuries to provide fuel for domestic use. Peat is not yet regrowing over the cut-over areas.

A relict vertical edge from an old peat-cutting in Wester Ross.

A relict peat-cutting in Wester Ross. The hollow in the foreground was once filled with peat, as can be deduced from the relict vertical peat visible above the hollow. It can be seen that this peat-cutting area is distant from the settlement.

The remains of the High Bridge of Spean, built between 1736 and 1737 to take the Wade military road between Fort William and Fort Augustus over the River Spean. Before bridges, the Highlands would have been a difficult landscape to traverse.

Road bridges old and new at Dunbeath in Caithness. The old stone-arched bridges tend to have more aesthetic appeal than the modern concrete structures.

The modern A9 trunk road north of Drumochter Pass, with an associated cycle route. Note the rosebay willowherb and self-seeded conifers colonising the disturbed ground of the road edge, as discussed later in Case Study 3.

Transport links

Roads and bridges

Before the building of the first military roads by General Wade, which began in 1725, the mountainous areas of the Highlands were road-less, and, importantly, bridge-less, with many rivers impeding travel. Much of the land was rough and boggy, making any inland travel difficult. The sea was the main highway.

The Wade roads were not particularly suited to civilian travel, although Haldane tells us they were used by cattle drovers,[3] and it was only possible for wheeled vehicles successfully to traverse the Highlands after the completion of the road network overseen by Thomas Telford in the early 19th century. These were the 'Parliamentary Roads', created by an Act of Parliament, with half the costs paid for by the government and half by the owners of the land the roads were passing through. Today this would be called a 'public–private partnership'. Their construction was supervised by the Highland road engineer Joseph Mitchell, whose memoirs provide an excellent insight into all the problems encountered, such as the difficulties of extracting money from some landowners, the difficulties of finding contractors, and the problem that many of the workers would leave for a period, having to return to their crofts for important tasks such as peat-cutting and potato harvesting.[4]

These Parliamentary Roads enabled the first regular coach services from the Central Belt to Inverness. The Highlands were now becoming accessible to the outside world, both for people and ideas.[5]

Early roads tended to follow the landform and, if no longer used, have mostly merged back into the landscape. Modern roads, in contrast, are built with significant landform modification to ensure straight and level routes, and new roads are significantly wider than their predecessors. There has also been a changing aesthetic: the old roads hugged the landscape and their bridges could be works of art; modern roads make no concession and their concrete bridges are rarely things of beauty.

Steamships and canals

The coming of steamships to the Highlands for the first time enabled large numbers of people to visit the area in relative comfort. The Crinan Canal, which joins Loch Fyne to the west coast, shortened the journey by allowing boats to avoid the long route round the Kintyre Peninsula. The route was surveyed by the famous Scots engineer James Watt in 1771 and the canal itself opened in 1809. Although the landscape impact is localised, by allowing steamships quick passage to and from Glasgow it assisted the opening up of the West Highlands and Islands to the outside world for trade and people. Outsiders could now easily visit the area and tourism boomed.

The route of the Caledonian Canal linking the east and the west through the Great Glen was also first surveyed by James Watt, and completed under the supervision of Thomas Telford in 1822. Again, it allowed easier movement of people and trade across the Highlands.

Railways

During the Victorian era the coming of the railways opened up the Highlands to mass visitation. The Highland railway though the Grampians from Perth to Inverness opened in 1863, making it possible to travel from London to Inverness in less than a day. Its original route was via Grantown-on-Spey over Dava Moor to Forres and then westwards to Inverness. The shorter route via Slochd did not open until 1898.

The development of the road and rail infrastructure in the previously trackless uplands was an essential prerequisite of the subsequent development of the Highlands, which, inevitably, accelerated landscape change, including the loss of wildness.

A paddle steamer of the type that would have originally plied the western Highlands. The boat pictured is the *Maid of the Loch* on Loch Lomond. It enabled urban populations to experience the Highlands.

The Caledonian Canal, which dissects the Highlands, shown here with the swing-bridge crossing of the northern railway to Kyle of Lochalsh, Wick and Thurso.

Kyle of Lochalsh Station. This line terminated at Stromeferry when it opened in 1870. It was extended to Kyle of Lochalsh in 1897, which at that time had only half a dozen houses. It was the gateway to Skye and the Outer Hebrides.

Dykes, fencing and compartmentalisation

Stone field boundaries have been around since Neolithic times but field boundaries were not common, the livestock instead being managed communally by shepherding. Livestock were taken to the summer pastures or shielings to allow crops to be grown on the inbye land. But with the reorganisation of agriculture and crofting post-Culloden there was a marked increase in the construction of stone dykes. The inbye land was often surrounded by a hill dyke so that animals could be left on the rough grazing beyond without any danger of incursion into the crops.

Compartmentalisation of the wider landscape began with the erection of fences and dykes as sheep-farm boundaries in the 18th century. These often went over the summits of hills at over 900 metres in altitude. Hillwalkers today often encounter their rusting remains, even in remote locations. These fences were not lightweight: erecting

Stock fences on crofting land, those in the background marking the apportionment of Common Grazings. Note also the green improved pasture.

them involved carrying heavy loads of cast iron posts and wire to the highest tops, cold-chiselling holes in the rock and melting lead solder to anchor the posts. But no challenge was too big for the Victorians!

Compartmentalisation of the remaining wild areas through fencing continues unabated today. This can be to manage grazing, separate landholdings, protect woodland and scrub or for road safety. Particularly common nowadays are long lengths of high deer fencing surrounding new woodland and forestry schemes. Roadside fencing also subdivides the area: roadside deer fencing from Garve to Loch Maree in effect isolates the red deer in the northwest Highlands, preventing deer movement in or out of the area.

Disused Victorian sheep fences remain in the hills. It is likely that many of the miles and miles of new fencing will never be removed, littering the landscape into the future.

Dry-stone dykes were common in the landscape before wire fencing became available in the 19th century. This one marks the boundary of the church glebe in Gairloch.

The remains of an old stone dyke built high in the hills to separate grazings at the time sheep farming was introduced.

The first fences in the 19th century had cast iron posts. They were built throughout the Highlands to separate sheep grazings, even to the summits of hills. Although they have now fallen into disuse their remains are still visible.

A modern post-and-wire stock fence of the type used today to separate sheep grazings in the hills.

A high deer fence in Wester Ross that protects newly planted trees from being eaten by deer. With all the new plantations being created, these fences are becoming increasingly common and are, in effect, compartmentalising the landscape.

Most main roads have fences on either side, in this case a deer fence. This is for road safety reasons. Self-seeded trees, here Sitka spruce, often colonise the strip of disturbed ground between the fence and the road.

Creation of the Highland estates

Although there have been castles and strongholds in the Highlands since Pictish times (brochs), these were largely coastal or in the larger straths, and were in locations where defence from attack was a priority.

The parcelling up of the Highlands first into sheep farms and later into extensive shooting estates came about after the break-up of the clan system and the change to a landowning economy. Many of the original clan chiefs sold their land to raise money. The purchasers were often cash-rich industrialists from the south. The new owners managed the land for themselves and their friends, who would visit the Highlands during the shooting season for deer stalking and grouse shooting.

Large lodges were built for this seasonal influx of visitors, often in remote locations in the heart of the mountains, with associated access tracks, smaller lodges and stalking paths: paths were constructed to allow easy access for people and ponies into the high corries where the red deer were to be found. Before this period these areas would have

A typical Highland shooting lodge built to house those coming for the autumn deer-stalking season. Note also the surround of rhododendron, which is discussed later.

been trackless, and where inhabited there would have been turf houses and smaller shieling huts along the floor of the glens.

On some estates, particularly those still owned by the original families such as the Atholl Estate, land management practices based on novel ideas from the south were introduced. These included agricultural improvement of the better land on the glen floors, new plantation forests, and the creation of aesthetically designed landscapes around the castle or big house. The hills and glens were slowly becoming tamed.

In the areas where grouse shooting was a key aim, particularly the heather moors in the central and eastern Highlands, the moors became increasingly managed to benefit the grouse. For example, Lord Cockburn observed in 1838 that "there has been more burning of heather… than I remember to have seen before".[6] The burning of heather on a regular basis for the benefit of red grouse is discussed in Chapter 3. It is a practice that gives a patchwork pattern to the hills.

Sronlairig Lodge, a shooting lodge in the Monadhliath Mountains (the building has recently been demolished).

Associated with the shooting lodges was an array of buildings such as keepers' cottages, deer larders and kennels.

On some estates smaller shooting lodges were built for overnight stays in the remoter areas. In the previous sheep farming era some shepherds' cottages would also have been built.

A zigzag stalking path in Inverness-shire for people and ponies to reach the higher corries. In this case, the path exhibits gully erosion, having turned into a water course over the years.

Strips of heather burnt to give a greater variety of habitat for red grouse: old-growth heather for shelter and shorter heather to provide nutritious shoots for the grouse to graze.

A mosaic of heather burns of different ages in the eastern Cairngorms.

Agricultural improvement

The term 'improvement' is from a farmer's perspective, meaning improving the land to make it more productive for growing crops or livestock. On a small scale the practice started when farming was introduced to the Highlands, and would have involved improving the fertility of the land through drainage, ploughing and the addition of plant nutrients from animal dung, seaweed or shell-sand. In the western Highlands and Islands this has created a landscape of ridges and furrows (rig-and-furrow), often termed lazybeds (mentioned in Chapter 2); their pattern persists in the landscape long after the people have gone, and can be observed in locations now distant from any settlement.

Agricultural improvement on a large scale began in the 1700s, mirroring a pattern of such change across the whole of Britain. It was often associated with the removal of the existing tenant farmers and crofters, both in lowland Scotland and the Highlands;[7] they were either relocated to more marginal land or had to leave the area.

A silage field created out of moorland on the island of Gigha.

In the Highlands, the climate and soil conditions are largely unsuitable for growing crops, particularly arable crops, so scope for improvement is limited. However, there is potential in some areas such as the floors of the wider glens and straths, the foothills of the eastern Highlands, and Caithness and Orkney. Here, extensive areas of what was once heather moorland or native grassland have been converted to improved pasture using modern varieties of grasses more palatable to animals than their wild counterparts. These require the addition of artificial fertilisers, making them stand out bright green against the muted browns of the natural vegetation. This practice was at one time grant-aided by the government and, although common in the 1950s and 1960s, it has largely ceased today.

A particularly special landscape is that of the machair – the free-draining, flower-rich coastal grasslands of the Long Island, present because of the addition of calcium-rich shell-sand to the soil, whether by the wind or by us.

A farm in Wester Ross created in the 19th century by improving the native moorland vegetation.

A field created from moorland in east Sutherland.

There has been extensive conversion of moorland to improved pasture on Orkney, here visible across the Loch of Harray.

The bright green of improved pasture at Sullom Voe in Shetland. The green is from the use of fertilisers and modern varieties of rye grass, which enable a crop of silage to be taken. Note the oil terminal in the background.

The conversion of a raised bog to agricultural pasture at the Mòine Mhòr in Argyll, showing how peatlands can be lost to agriculture.

A fence line on the island of Unst, Shetland, showing the improved pasture on the left and native vegetation on the right; improved pastures are always a brighter green.

Forest plantations

Trees were first planted in the Highlands by landowners from the end of the 18th century. When the poet Robert Burns visited the Falls of Bruar in Perthshire in 1787 the landscape was unwooded. Burns felt it would be improved by the addition of trees, so much so that he wrote a poem to that effect, 'The Humble Petition Of Bruar Water'. Burns' desire shows how we like to shape the landscape to fit in with our own aesthetic preferences, wanting to improve what we have inherited from nature. Later, the owner, the Duke of Atholl, did plant trees but when the poet William Wordsworth and his sister Dorothy visited the falls in 1903 he criticised the duke's plantings:[8]

Glen Lochy, through which the trunk road to Oban passes. Most of the glen floor and all the lower slopes have given way to commercial forestry.

We walked upwards at least three quarters of a mile in the hot sun, with the stream on our right, both sides of which to a considerable height were planted with firs and larches intermingled – children of poor Burns' song; for his sake we wished that they had been the natural trees of Scotland, birches, ashes, mountain ashes, etc., however, sixty or seventy years from now they will be no unworthy monument to his memory.

However, James Robertson in 1771, when in the Grantown-on-Spey area, was pleased to see the plantations around Castle Grant:[9]

Early plantings by landowners were often for amenity reasons, adding an aesthetic around the big house or creating woodland walks. These were designed landscapes, such as at the Inveraray Estate above. Some plantations were for timber for estate use.

The UK-wide Forestry Commission, headquartered in Scotland, was set up in 1919 to create a strategic reserve of timber. It is the only example in the UK of the state buying land from private owners on a large scale.

Whole sheep farms were bought out, the above being an example in the Galloway Hills of southern Scotland; only the best land around the farmhouse has been left unplanted.

Whole landscapes became covered in trees – 'blanket forestry'. It is uniform at first, but once felling starts after about 60 years the landscape becomes a mosaic of mature trees, felled areas and young plantations.

The main tree planted nowadays in commercial forests in the Highlands is the Sitka spruce from North America. The above shows a planting on relatively gentle slopes which, from a carbon sequestration perspective, might be best left unplanted.

Generally it is the glen floors and lower slopes of the hills that are planted, here on the Island of Mull. These are the locations most suited to carbon sequestration by the soil or peat if left unplanted. Straight-line edges were characteristic of earlier plantings, but nowadays trees are planted to better fit into the landscape.

> Were all the Gentlemen of the North to imitate Mr Grant [proprietor of the castle], the happiest consequences might be expected from their exertions. Instead of naked hills & dreary mosses, the eye would then survey with pleasure, woody or verdant mountains raising their heads above cultivated fields, while the industrious Tenant, tho' his rent were tripled, would live better than he does at present, & be under no temptation to quit his native land.

This is perhaps the first mention of the belief, now espoused by many environmentalists, that trees are the answer to all our woes.

Until recent years, the choice of trees in the plantations springing up around the Highlands was not based on the trees naturally present but was determined largely by aesthetic or commercial considerations. The new woods being planted did not match the characteristics of the remaining native Highland woodlands, and introduced an ecological discontinuity, something that continues to this day.

People rightly condemn the loss of natural vegetation in the Amazon Basin (tropical rainforest) and its replacement with non-indigenous pasture and crops; indeed there is a global outcry about it. But why is there not such an outcry when large tracts of natural Highland vegetation (open moorland), much of which is recognised with international labels, is converted to plantations of non-indigenous trees? Is it because most people think, incorrectly, that the Highland landscape is not natural in the first place? In which case we are allowing its destruction through ignorance.

Tree planting was originally undertaken by private landowners with an interest in forestry and has been well described in Smout's book *People and Woods in Scotland: A History*.[10] However, after the First World War most tree planting was carried out by the state under the auspices of the Forestry Commission, set up in 1919 to create a strategic national reserve of timber, it being realised during the war that the country was overly dependent on imported wood. The Commission bought up private land, particularly when sheep farming was in a depressed state, and in places whole sheep farms would be planted, particularly in Argyll.

Large tracts of the landscape would be transformed, creating what would later be termed 'blanket forestry'. In the early years a wide range of conifers were planted, including the native Scots pine, but mostly it was conifers from other parts of the world such as Norway spruce, Sitka spruce, various firs, lodge pole pine and western hemlock. In later years the focus has almost entirely been on Sitka spruce from the Sitka region of western North America. This tree grows well in the Scottish climate and thrives on the acid, infertile soils characteristic of the area.

It was soon recognised that the trees would establish more quickly and grow faster if the soil was ploughed, which dries out the soil, breaks up the iron pan and allows the tree roots access to mineral-rich areas below. Often fertiliser is added in the early years, which also accelerates tree growth. The plough lines result in irreversible change, destroying at a stroke 10,000 years' worth of soil development. The native vegetation will

The quickest way to establish forests is to plough the land, a highly destructive practice. This results in permanent landscape scarring: the plough lines remain even if the trees are removed.

The practice dries out the soil, which is good for the trees but bad for the climate: the soil carbon is exposed to the air and oxidises away. Here recent ploughing in Argyll.

When the forests are mature, after about 60 years, they are clear-felled: if left to get old, in Scotland's windy climate there is a risk of all the trees blowing over. Note some windthrow at the edge of the clear-felled area.

During extraction the soil is disturbed by heavy machinery, releasing more soil carbon. It can never be said that clear-fell sites are places of beauty.

Forestry is a highly mechanised industry and in effect is industrialisation of the landscape.

Major tracks are constructed to allow access to the forty-tonne timber lorries necessary to take the timber away for processing.

never return, even if harvested trees are not replaced. The regular pattern of ridges and hollows will also remain for thousands of years.

Associated with the tree planting is the construction of tall, unsightly fences to keep out deer, the killing of any deer within the fenced enclosures, and the construction of vehicle tracks to allow access for tree planting and harvesting. Forestry tracks have become increasingly wide and heavily engineered in recent years to allow access for large timber lorries. The trees are felled after about sixty years over large areas all at once: if left longer, or felled individually, some trees may blow over. Areas of trees felled by the wind are often visible on the edges of forests and clear-fell sites, and within the forest itself. Felling involves the use of large machinery, which churns up the soil. The dense canopy of mature conifers will have already shaded out and killed any vegetation beneath and the plants which thereafter colonise the disturbed ground are very different from those which grew before tree planting. Finally, machines are used to pile up the brash – the cut-off branches – in straight lines to make it easier to plant the next generation of trees.

Another problem is that the now extensive commercial forests provide ideal habitat for the introduced sika deer from Japan. These are spreading throughout the Highlands and interbreed with native red deer. In time, there may be no genetically-pure red deer left on the mainland.

Modern forestry does provide much needed jobs in rural areas but it is also one of the most damaging and irreversible practices impacting the land. It is an industrial process at odds with keeping any vestiges of the traditional Highland landscape. As will be seen in Case Study 2, it is also causing long-term and more insidious landscape change through the plantation conifers spreading to the wider countryside.

CASE STUDY 1

The ecological impact of disturbing Highland soils

The cross-section of a typical Highland unmixed and stratified soil (a podsol). Note that the organic matter from dead plant remains is all at the surface because the soil is too acidic and wet for earthworms to be present. The minerals (including plant nutrients) have been leached downwards by rainfall and are unavailable to plant roots owing to the impermeable iron pan (dark orange, see below). The iron pan also prevents water draining down into the soil, resulting in a tendency for waterlogging.

The iron pan is visible as a layer of iron in the centre of the photograph. It was sometimes mined for its iron, known as 'bog iron'. The orange colour is from the iron (rust).

The rocks of the Highlands result in generally infertile soils. The presence of limestone can result in localised areas of more fertile soils with no iron pan. The greener area above, near Kishorn in Wester Ross, is underlain by Jurassic limestone

Forest ploughing of a whole landscape of heather moor to assist the establishment of a planted Scots pine woodland on Dava Moor in Moray. The mineral soil is brought to the surface, resulting in irreversible changes to the soil.

The two stripes of paler vegetation are where a water main and telephone line were buried about forty years ago. The soil disturbance, including breaking through the iron pan, is resulting in different vegetation. The white plant is predominantly mat grass.

The soil along the road here was disturbed during road improvements in the 1970s. The better drained area nearest the road is dominated by grass and is being colonised by gorse. Rushes now dominate the disturbed damper areas. See also the lower picture of p. 17.

After planting and then felling a forest, the soil is irreversibly changed: in effect it is being returned to its state in the mesocratic phase of postglacial succession. The foxgloves above would not have been in the original moorland.

Thistles colonising disturbed ground caused by construction of a track and power station for a run-of-river hydro-electric scheme near Braemar. Disturbed ground is colonised by a different array of species than the native vegetation.

A felled plantation above Loch Cluanie. The felled area will have different vegetation to the unplanted surrounding moorland for hundreds of years.

CASE STUDY 2
Self-seeding Sitka spruce

Early-stage colonisation of the landscape by Sitka spruce seeding-out from a commercial plantation at the Rest and Be Thankful pass in Argyll. In the windy climate, the seeds can blow a long way. Unlike rhododendron, the tree dies when cut down, but there is no incentive for landowners to remove trees seeding-out from their plantations. Over time, colonisation by Sitka spruce will completely transform the Highland landscape, turning the whole area into a forest of spruce.

Spruce leaping over the plantation fence to colonise the wider countryside.

Young spruce colonising a native birch wood.

Early-stage colonisation of moorland in Argyll.

Early-stage colonisation of a lowland peat bog in Argyll.

Early-stage colonisation of mid-altitude blanket peat in Inverness-shire.

Seeding-out of spruce onto moorland from the commercial plantation below.

Conifers invading moorland in Wester Ross adjacent to the plantation in the foreground, in this case mainly lodgepole pine.

The disturbed ground at the edge of roads and tracks provides a seedbed for spruce and other trees, which is why self-seeded spruce is common alongside many roads. Spruce is versatile and is also able to colonise areas with undisturbed soils.

The original hydro-electric schemes

Construction of the first large-scale hydro-electric scheme in Britain began in 1895 at Foyers on the shores of Loch Ness to provide power for aluminium smelting. Other schemes involved the conversion of lochs into reservoirs, the creation of tunnels and the building of power stations in Kinlochleven and Fort William.

In the 1930s the Galloway Power Scheme was built in the Glenkens and Loch Doon area of southern Scotland. Loch Doon was converted into a reservoir, dams were built along the Water of Ken from Carsphairn to Kirkcudbright, and a new loch was created in the hills at Clatteringshaws. In fact nearly all the landscape changes discussed in this book have also occurred in the Galloway Hills, where there have been even more forest plantations created and loss of wild land than in the Highlands. The Tummel-Garry hydro-electric scheme in the Highlands was also built in this interwar period.

Tom Johnston, the Secretary of State for Scotland in Winston Churchill's cabinet during the Second World War, had a vision of bringing 'Power to the Glens', the aim being to stimulate the Highland economy by providing cheap power. Economic development has always been hard to achieve in the Highlands, with well-paid jobs few and far between. So, with the formation of the North of Scotland Hydro-Electric Board in 1943, another era of dam building began.

The Ben Cruachan dam, a pumped-storage scheme associated with Loch Awe below, was built high in the mountains.

The building of these schemes for a while converted remote areas into industrial sites, although most of the landscape scars have now healed. However, the dams themselves remain visible.

A tailings heap and pipe associated with the hydro scheme above Loch Tay. This view represents a modern Highland landscape of energy generation and commercial forestry plantation.

It was a massive undertaking over many years and the end result in 1965 was a total of 78 dams, 54 power stations and over 300km of underground tunnels.[11] Over half of the river catchments of the Highlands were now tamed for hydro schemes. There were some objections, particularly from fishing interests, many of which were overcome by the building of fish passes and agreement that at least some water would remain flowing in the dammed rivers (the so-called 'compensation flow'). Other objections were on landscape grounds: the flooding of the Linn of Tummel to create Loch Faskally in Pitlochry was mourned. An earlier scheme for Glen Affric, long renowned for its beauty, was modified so that Loch Affric itself remained undammed. There were also strong objections to the proposed Glen Nevis scheme, which in the event was never built. Another scheme exploiting Loch Maree in an area of Wester Ross famed for its scenery was also abandoned as was the one below Ben Lomond. However, most politicians and the public in the Highlands welcomed the dams and power stations as a boost to both quality of life and economic development – see the quote on p. 3.

Long-term landscape impact in addition to the concrete dam included the damming of many tributary burns to feed water into the reservoirs, tailings heaps, quarries, the creation of new roads, large, visible overground pipes in some areas, power stations and power lines. The water levels in the reservoirs rises and falls to a much greater extent than in the original lochs, dependent on the amount of rainfall and the demand for electricity. The loch shore between the highest and lowest water levels, termed the 'drawdown zone', is generally devoid of vegetation because few plants can survive being flooded and then dry for long periods; additionally, wave action washes out any fine soil or silt. When water levels are low the unvegetated drawdown zone is strikingly visible, the rocks along the shore having no lichens growing on them to mask their colour.

Most of the easily exploitable catchments in the Highlands have been developed, so new ones tend to be small-scale 'run-of-river' schemes. These are discussed later. There are, though, plans for new pumped-storage schemes in the Highlands, which will involve creating reservoirs high in the hills similar to the Glendoe scheme above Fort Augustus built in 2008, and the earlier Cruachan scheme. It is worth noting that all the large-scale hydro schemes in the Highlands provide only about ten per cent of Scotland's electricity needs, and the potential for new ones is low: hydroelectricity can only have a limited role in solving Scotland's energy needs.

An aqueduct associated with a hydro scheme in Perthshire.

The Loch Cluanie dam with the reservoir at low level, making the drawdown zone highly visible. This is the area that Lord Cockburn eulogised for its wildness in 1841.

Another picture of Loch Cluanie showing how the reservoirs created have a highly visible drawdown zone around their edges when the water levels are low. This distinguishes them from natural lochs where the rise and fall is less extreme.

Transmission lines and masts

Power generated within the Highland landscape has to be exported to where it is needed. Pylons carrying the electricity through the hills are now so part of the landscape that we barely notice them.

With all the new energy being produced from the windfarms, the original electricity grid has become too small. Lines are being upgraded with larger and taller pylons, even through areas perceived as being of high landscape appeal such as along the A9 trunk road through Drumochter Pass. This is because society is not prepared to pay the extra cost of putting the power lines underground, perhaps indicating a lack of value placed

Electrical infrastructure associated with the Ben Cruachan pumped-storage hydro-electric scheme in Argyll. A track up the glen is visible in the background.

on the landscape – economic development, understandingly, always being a higher priority. A recent exception to this is on the island of Skye where there are plans to bury the electricity cables in the vicinity of the iconic Cuillin hills.

On a smaller scale than the electricity poles and pylons, mobile phone masts have sprung up across the Highlands since the 1990s. These have to be in relatively prominent positions to maximise the spread of the phone signals and can be seen even along remote routes. Access is required to these for maintenance, necessitating either bulldozed tracks or cross-country routes liable to erosion: yet more incursions by infrastructure.

Electricity transmission lines are now a common part of the landscape.

The number of transmission lines is increasing through the development of hydro-electric schemes and windfarms.

The corridor of the A9 trunk road near Dalwhinnie, showing the pylons of the national grid that enable the electricity generated to be exported to the south. The original pylons have been replaced in recent years with the taller ones here.

As well as the large metal pylons there is a widespread network of lower-voltage power lines that use wooden poles. The one illustrated here is associated with the River Grudie run-of-river hydro scheme near Loch Maree in Wester Ross.

A mobile phone mast above Loch Cluanie in Inverness-shire.

A hilltop telecommunications mast and associated infrastructure.

Footpaths

The creation of stalking paths on shooting estates has already been mentioned. However, these paths led into the corries, where the deer were to be found, rather than to the summits of the hills. With the advent of hill climbing as a pastime, other paths developed along popular routes. A few were constructed, such as the path up Ben Nevis for access to the Observatory on the summit, which opened in 1883, but most were not planned. Hence there has arisen an informal path network to the summits and this path network is still expanding today. Some paths have also developed recently to destinations made popular by films and social media, such as the Fairy Pools or Old Man of Storr on Skye.

A new footpath taking people to the Fairy Pools on the Isle of Skye, a location made popular by social media.

Because these paths are not formally constructed they are subject to water erosion in the wet Highland climate, and can enlarge to become scars on the landscape. Teams of skilled footpath workers install drains, make the paths more resistant to erosion, and revegetate eroding areas. This makes the previously rough paths easier to walk along. In the same way that the creation of roads eased access to the Highlands, these new paths are allowing walkers easy access to previously pathless land.

The footpath up Mount Keen in Aberdeenshire, the easternmost Munro (hill over 3,000 feet in height), which stands out in the landscape. A water-caused gully can be seen. Picture taken in 1998.

Another site of gully erosion on the Mount Keen path. The summit is in the background. Picture taken in 1998.

Erosion in 1995 along the path up the popular hill Stac Pollaidh. Walkers are now avoiding the gully by traversing the vegetated area to the left, which will itself erode, causing the whole path to widen and an erosion scar to form.

Another section of the path up Stac Pollaidh in Wester Ross, which has been improved to prevent erosion. Picture taken in 1995.

The summit of Ben Doran above Bridge of Orchy. All Munros now have a path to the summit, most of which were not built but have evolved over time. Most of these paths are subject to erosion in places.

A once-eroded path in Glencoe, which has been improved to prevent the once-widespread erosion here. Such improvements, while preventing erosion, do make access into the hills easier.

Bulldozed tracks

No activity can take place in the hills these days without the construction of access tracks for vehicles. The justification is normally economic, along the lines of 'we can't carry out this essential activity unless we can use vehicles'. Access is said to be required for diverse reasons, including tree planting and harvesting, managing sheep and livestock, getting into the hills for deer stalking and grouse shooting, hydro-electric schemes, windfarms, access to phone masts and pylons, and ski development.

Some of the latest tracks can be six metres wide, especially those for forestry operations and windfarm construction, and can involve major engineering. There are also tracks yet to be built: the trees in many of the extensive new woodlands have been planted without the need for engineered tracks, but new tracks will be needed for harvesting. Or the trees can just be left to blow over!

Walking along a track through a commercial plantation is the same experience, whether in Wales or Wester Ross, Galloway or the Grampians, and is another example of the general homogenisation of landscapes.

The endpoint of all this is that nowadays it is very difficult to find anywhere in the Highlands more than a mile or two from a track. Often a footpath has been transformed

An old stalking path up a glen that has been converted into a vehicle track.

into a track, and sometimes extended into a new area. There are in effect no controls on the process, landowners and developers in practice being allowed to build tracks anywhere they wish.

Some tracks are badly built and many are not maintained to a high standard, or are too steep, so that water erosion sets in. Many represent an irreversible change to the landscape: in theory it is possible to remove them and restore the original landform, but this is difficult in practice and probably more expensive than building the track in the first place – which perhaps only required one person and a digger. To its credit, the National Trust for Scotland has removed an unnecessary track up Beinn a' Bhuird in the eastern Cairngorms – but this is the exception rather than the rule.

All these tracks must be the ultimate taming of the Highlands: everywhere accessible to all people at all times! The long-term ecological impact of bulldozing such tracks is discussed in Case Study 3, the disturbed ground becoming a corridor for the invasion by species not indigenous to the area.

Most glens now seem to have a vehicle track running their length. Some have been converted from footpaths, others are newly created.

A recently bulldozed track in Argyll to provide access for deer stalking.

A bulldozed track in the Monadhliath Mountains to provide access for stalking and grouse shooting. Note the drainage gully dug in the peat, which is likely to erode, and the disturbed ground on the right, which is likely to be colonised by a variety of plants.

A badly built track currently washing away. Drainage pipes need to be built in the right place and both the side ditches and pipes need to be regularly cleared of any rocks and stones – something which does not always happen.

A large track built by the Forestry Commission in Glen Lochy to allow timber harvesting. This is a new forest road parallel to the existing public road. New private road networks for forestry and windfarms are becoming increasingly common.

The access track to the large Glensanda Quarry on the north side of Loch Linnhe.

CASE STUDY 3
The ecological impact of tracks and roads

A track built through blanket peat at 500 metres altitude to access a windfarm in the Monadhliath Mountains. Although the disturbed ground along the edges was reseeded and has now revegetated, the species used are different to those of the surrounding peat. This disturbed soil now provides a corridor of invasion for species that are otherwise absent in the area, as shown below.

The rush *Juncus effusus* is colonising the edge of the track illustrated above. It is not otherwise present in this area of blanket peat.

Gorse and broom colonising the sides of a forestry track in Wester Ross. See also Case Study 7 on the spread of gorse.

It is not only roads and tracks that provide conduits for invasion: here the northern railway to Wick and Thurso is introducing gorse into the Flow Country.

It can be seen here that young conifers are successfully colonising the disturbed ground of an old track, whereas the old growth heather is relatively resistant to tree invasion.

The disturbed ground along roads, tracks and paths provides an ideal seedbed for trees; here Sitka spruce has spread from the surrounding plantation.

Larch and spruce seeding-out from the plantation on the right to colonise the disturbed ground on both sides of the road through Strath Bran.

Following road improvement down Glen Docherty, trees (both native and escaped conifers) are colonising the area between the road and the fences. In time there will be linear belt of trees down the glen, a famous viewpoint to Loch Maree.

Rosebay willowherb has here colonised the sides of the A9 trunk road and associated cycle path north of Drumochter Pass. It is a plant previously absent from this moorland. Self-seeded conifers are also common along this stretch of road.

Downhill ski resorts

Downhill skiing took off in the early 20th century and perhaps the most popular area for the early ski enthusiasts in Scotland was Coire Odhar on Ben Lawers, where a ski hut was built.

The first permanent ski tow was built in 1956 on Meall a' Bhùiridh at the eastern end of Glencoe. Further resorts were developed at Cairngorm, Glenshee and The Lecht, and finally in 1988 of Aonach Mor above Fort William in 1988. The resorts expanded through the addition of more ski lifts. The last major construction was the building in 2001 of the funicular railway up Cairn Gorm,[12] the sixth highest mountain in Scotland.

Ski resorts involve the creation of considerable infrastructure such as car parks, buildings, ski lifts, snow fencing and vehicle tracks up the hill for maintenance and access. Hence their impact on the landscape is high.

Scotland has always been marginal for consistent winter snow cover. The 1960s, when most resorts were developed, was a period of colder winters than average with good skiing to be had most years. Since then the climate has returned to perhaps a more normal pattern of alternating cold winters and mild winters, making the economics of running resorts particularly fragile; this situation is only likely to worsen with global warming.

Resorts therefore are trying to widen their range of activities, encouraging both the summer tourist into the hills and developing downhill mountain biking as an alternative to skiing, which can involve the construction of new cycle paths. The hills are now seen by many not as places to enjoy in their own right, but as places for self-centred adventure and challenge – to seek the adrenalin rush that goes with intense activity. Perhaps they are now seen by many as mere theme parks.

The Nevis Range ski area on Aonach Mor, 650–1,200 metres altitude.

The Cairngorm ski area showing the funicular railway with its concrete pillars, ski tows, snow fences and buildings.

The top of the Cairngorm ski area at 1,000 metres altitude on a busy day.

Infrastructure at 800 metres altitude associated with downhill skiing at Cairngorm.

The Glencoe ski area on Meall a' Bhùiridh, altitude 850 metres.

The Glenshee ski centre in summer, altitude 700 metres. Note the extensive car park along the main road.

The car park at Cairngorm, altitude 600 metres.

Wheel marks

With the advent of all-terrain vehicles in the 1960s and more recently quad bikes, land managers have increasingly been using vehicles to take themselves off any formal tracks into the hills. This can be for managing sheep, assisting deer stalking and deer culls, access to grouse moors, access to distant lochs for fishing, access to masts and energy infrastructure, and for general recreational use.

The resulting wheel marks are often visible in the vegetation and, as with footpaths, can instigate erosion, particularly where the soils are soft and peaty. Such marks can often be seen on hill tops even in remote areas, reducing the sense of wildness and adding

Wheel marks from all-terrain vehicles accessing Lairig Gartain in Glencoe, to allow conservation deer culls to take place. Here, culling the deer in the name of conservation is creating landscape damage.

the obvious human hand to previously unsullied areas. Ease of access is prioritised over landscape damage.

The development of such informal vehicle routes with the associated erosion can lead to the landowner turning the route into a bulldozed vehicle track. A recent development is the increasing prevalence of off-road bicycling, often with electric bikes, with resultant wheel marks in the landscape. Remote glens and hills are being brought into the world of ever-easier access.

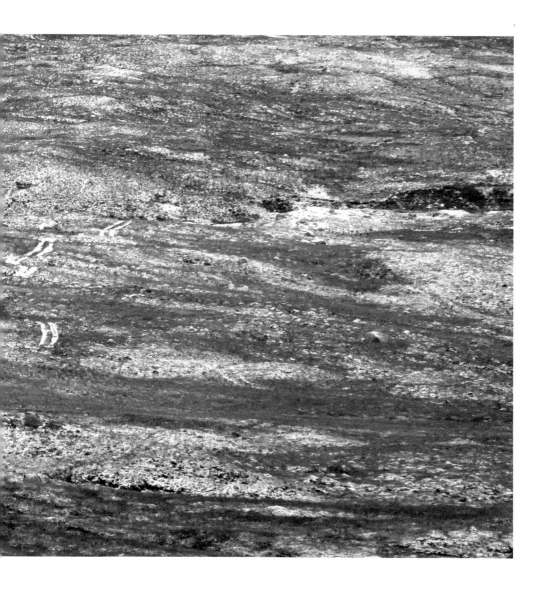

A close-up of the Lairig Gartain tracks, showing how the wheel marks have concentrated the water flow leading to incipient gully erosion.

Vehicle tracks at 750 metres altitude beside an old dyke built to separate sheep grazings.

Peat erosion being caused by quad bikes used to access sheep in a Common Grazings in Wester Ross.

A nearby route showing the first stage of peat erosion.

The same route showing, in the distance, how it has become converted to a more formal track. This illustrates how vehicle access to previously remote areas is often the first step to the creation of formalised vehicle tracks, their creation justified as an erosion prevention measure.

Landscape damage in Wester Ross from vehicles accessing a phone mast which has no formalised access track.

Windfarms

Windfarms are a characteristic feature of the 21st-century landscape. It is almost as if they sprang out of nowhere in the 1990s and soon covered many hill tops. The process came about so quickly that Scotland was not ready with any strategic plan for where they should be put. The main determinant has instead been a willing landowner and nearness to the national electricity grid. However the government has since determined that they should not be located in areas noted for their iconic scenery, in particular within National Parks and within those landscapes designated as National Scenic Areas.

The tall turbines are generally visible from multiple viewpoints and with each new generation their height increases, soon, perhaps, to be over 200 metres (650 feet) from ground to blade tip. However their visual impact is reversible in that they can be taken down, but the associated infrastructure can result in permanent landscape change. Their construction necessitates the creation of a network of access tracks, often of long distance, which require large volumes of hardcore as foundation, either from local borrow pits or imported. Turbine foundations use considerable amounts of concrete (as did the original hydro-electric schemes). At the end of a windfarm's life it is theoretically

The Farr windfarm in the Monadhliath Mountains south of Inverness.

possible to remove the tracks, concrete foundations and imported hardcore to reinstate the original landform, but this is an expensive operation and probably not practical.

The Scottish hills are erosive environments and the concrete foundations will be there for thousands of years to come even if the windfarms are long gone: indeed, the blocks may come to the surface if the surrounding soil or peat erodes away. The legacy of the oil industry in Alaska will be the infrastructure left behind. The legacy of Highland windfarms will be the same, much like the lines of concrete blocks along east coast beaches put in place as tank traps during the Second World War, although it is of course possible that the windfarms will be forever there.

When downwind of a large windfarm you sometimes hear a roar akin to that of a distant motorway, although gently rotating turbines do have a certain aesthetic appeal, perhaps enhanced by the knowledge that they are helping to save the planet. There is no doubt, though, that their presence does represent the continuing industrialisation of the hills and moors, causing the original wildness to retreat into the ever-decreasing mountain fastnesses.

The Novar windfarm in Easter Ross. Note the constructed vehicle tracks giving access to every turbine. Extensive networks of vehicle tracks are part and parcel of every windfarm.

Wind turbines in Argyll with Ben Cruachan in the background.

Part of the 40-turbine Farr windfarm in winter.

The Farr windfarm, built within a blanket peat landscape. Note the wide access tracks, the hardstanding at the base of the tower and the people for scale. Each tower will have a large concrete foundation buried beneath.

The Farr windfarm showing access tracks and in the middle distance a quarry to provide hardcore for the tracks and hardstandings. In this photograph the quarry sides are being reprofiled and covered with soil (peat) to allow revegetation.

Concrete blocks from the Second World War used as tank traps along the coast of Moray. The concrete foundations for wind turbines are an order of magnitude bigger and will persist in the landscape long after all the turbines have gone.

New woods of native trees

The creation of new plantations in the Highlands, particularly the planting of commercial forests by the Forestry Commission, has already been discussed. But in recent years plantations of native trees have increasingly been planted for conservation reasons, based on the premise that there was once a Great Forest of Caledon which we humans have destroyed (as discussed in Chapter 3). The process was accelerated by the Millennium Forest for Scotland, an initiative at the turn of the century to promote the planting of native trees.

In fact it is not only the planting of trees within fenced enclosures that has occurred – deer are an ever-present threat to such forests – but also the encouragement of the seeding-out of trees from existing indigenous woods without the use of fences. For this, the number of deer must be reduced. This approach is termed 'natural regeneration' but there is nothing natural in forcing such low grazing levels onto the landscape, although it is true that humans are not determining the exact locations of individual trees.

Associated with new plantings is the deer fence and ground preparation. The commonest way of doing this is mounding, although ploughing and notch-planting can also be used, the latter using a spade to push apart the soil. Mounding and ploughing involve destroying thousands of years of soil development.

The creation of these woods, like the commercial plantations, is breaking the continuous ecological link back to the Ice Age: previously no human had determined the vegetation pattern of the landscape; it was left to nature. These plantations are helping to destroy the wildness of the Highlands.

These woods are often planted without the creation of a bulldozed access track, although wheel marks are often left. But tracks will be needed if the woods are ever to be harvested. Otherwise, many of the trees, when mature, will blow over: they tend to be shallow-rooted and the Highlands has a windy climate.

Some of these plantations have been created in places ecologically unsuited to trees, causing many to die or become thin and straggly. They have been grant-aided by government – surely a waste of taxpayer's money?

All plantations impact the grazing available for native red deer. As trees slowly fill the landscape, the natural grazing pattern of the deer is upset. The deer naturally spend their time in the high corries during the day, coming down to the flats at night. New fences can block their routes or channel them into narrow corridors, and much of the grazing can become inaccessible, for deer are not allowed into the new woods, even though we are told that red deer are woodland animals. Any deer that get into the plantations are shot. There is a welfare issue here.

See Case Study 4 on issues associated with new woods of native trees.

A new plantation of Scots pine and native broadleaved trees in Glen Nevis.

A new plantation of Scots pine at Loch Bad an Sgalaig in Wester Ross.

A new plantation of native trees near Kingairloch north of Loch Linnhe.

A new plantation of Scots pine near Achnasheen in Wester Ross, planted mainly on blanket peat.

A new plantation of native trees in Glen Shiel. Note that the plantation has been enclosed by a deer fence allowing the heather to grow taller than in the grazed area outside the fence.

A new plantation of Scots pine on heather moorland at Dava Moor in Moray.

CASE STUDY 4

Issues associated with new woods of native trees

A new plantation of native Scots pine, planted on heather moorland in the Cairngorms at an altitude of 600 metres. The habitat the trees are planted on, heather moorland, is much rarer globally than Scots pine woodland. The trees are planted close together, so when mature they will be tall and skinny: they will not have the aesthetic, wide-crowned canopies of the 'granny pines' shown below. Native woodland is unlikely to have been present in this locality for thousands of years, having declined naturally over the centuries.

Dense regeneration of native pine in Glen Feshie brought about by reducing the deer population to far below any expected natural level. Trees are regenerating at a density which will not result in many wide-crowned mature trees.

Native Scots pine planted near the relict native pine forest of Glas Leitire in Wester Ross. The trees are planted close together and the ground flora is dominated by purple moor grass, which has replaced the original, more species-rich moorland.

A 150-year-old plantation of Scots pine and larch in Wester Ross showing what many of the new plantations will look like in the future: tall, leggy trees that eventually blow over.

These Scots pines were planted about 15 years ago and are now in a poor state, with many dying. This is commonly the case for plantations in the west of the Highlands. The trees tend to be more healthy when planted in the east Highlands.

Another plantation in Wester Ross, about 20 years old, where most of the trees are unhealthy or dead. The benefits of plantations such as these has to be questioned. Compare these with the healthy young trees shown in the first picture on p. 133.

This whole landscape was mounded and planted with thousands of trees, none of which has survived. The scheme was billed as one of the largest new native woods in Scotland. All that is left in this part is damaged soil from mounding.

Mounding of the ground by a digger to create a new plantation of native trees above Loch Torridon. As with forestry ploughing, this destroys 10,000 years of soil development.

A new plantation near Achnasheen in Wester Ross where most of the trees are on blanket peat and humus-rich moorland. The trees are not particularly healthy and from a climate perspective it would be better to have left the peatland intact.

Run-of-river hydro-electric schemes

In the same way that windfarms exploded onto the scene with little warning, suddenly it seems that run-of-river schemes are everywhere and that every glen has a new bulldozed track up to a dam, from which the burn has the indignity of being piped underground to a new power station below. This has happened without any public debate, and the first you know of it is when you see mechanical diggers in your favourite glen.

Run-of-river schemes do not require large reservoirs but rely on the natural flow of water down a burn or river on any given day. A small dam traps the water and channels

Construction associated with a run-of-river hydro-electric scheme above Glen Falloch within the Loch Lomond & The Trossachs National Park.

it into a pipe. These dams can fill with boulders and gravel during spates, so permanent access is needed to clear them out. Hence the access track.

These schemes may be smaller in scale than the original hydro schemes of the 1950s and 1960s, but they are dispersed, so it is becoming increasingly difficult to find a glen with a wild, untamed river as nature intended and without a vehicle track. These tracks, like all tracks, create corridors of disturbed ground that allow entry of species not otherwise in the locality.

See Case Studies 5 and 6 on the River Grudie hydro-electric scheme.

A new bulldozed track up a glen to a dam for a run-of-river hydro-electric scheme in Ardgour, a common situation in numerous glens across the Highlands.

A track to a dam for a run-of-river scheme in Kingairloch, Morvern. The power station is visible at the bottom. All such schemes share a dam, a buried pipe (causing soil disturbance), a track and a power station.

A concrete dam associated with a small hydro-electric scheme in the Wester Ross National Scenic Area.

Another dam associated with a small scheme in Wester Ross.

A concrete water intake for a small scheme near Braemar. Note the associated rock armouring downstream of the dam, resulting in an artificial-looking bank to the burn.

A relatively unobtrusive scheme within a forestry plantation in Glenorchy.

CASE STUDY 5

Landscape impact of the River Grudie hydro-electric scheme in Wester Ross

The River Grudie flows northwards out of the heart of the Torridon mountains into Loch Maree. The Torridon mountains represent one of the few remaining trackless mountain massifs in the Highlands. The area has been designated by NatureScot a Wild Land Area. Its spectacular landscape has long been recognised as iconic and the area was recommended for National Park status by the Ramsay Committee in 1945. It retained the designation of National Park Direction Area until designated a National Scenic Area in 1982. It is currently within the Wester Ross Biosphere. The glen above is adjacent to the Beinn Eighe National Nature Reserve. This picture shows work on building the hydro scheme in 2016, with the access track visible up the glen.

The power house and transmission lines. Although the building has been landscaped into the ground from the west, it is visible from the east. The disturbed ground around the construction will be colonised by non-local plants.

The dam in the heart of the mountains showing all the disturbed ground where the pipe has been buried. The picture was taken in 2017 before the disturbed area had revegetated.

The dam, the new reservoir and associated deer fencing.

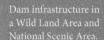

Dam infrastructure in a Wild Land Area and National Scenic Area.

The new track from the power station to the dam five years after construction. The paler vegetation along the tracks indicates where the pipe from the dam to the power station has been buried. This track makes access easier into a wild area.

A canalised burn with a plastic pipe under the track and visible polythene sheeting. A deer fence is just visible in the top left of the photograph.

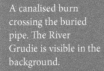

A canalised burn crossing the buried pipe. The River Grudie is visible in the background.

The deer fence and gates associated with the tree planting around the reservoir are intrusions into a wild, previously fenceless area.

CASE STUDY 6

Ecological impact of the River Grudie hydro-electric scheme in Wester Ross

The paler vegetation parallel to the track illustrates the extent of the ground disturbed during the construction. The soil now has a different structure to that of the surrounding vegetation and hence a different array of species, with grasses, in particular, more common; see also case studies 1 and 3. It is an ideal invasion corridor for gorse and other plants. Along the banks of the river are old Scots pine trees, with the river gorge on the right being particularly wooded. There are no trees away from the river's edge.

Gorse, visible right, has colonised the sides of the main road along Loch Maree; this has been a source of seed for colonisation of the start of the access track to the power station and dam, visible left. Note also the planted conifers to the left.

A young gorse bush is visible to the left of the track, the next stage of a probable colonisation of gorse along the disturbed ground all the way up to the dam: see also Case Study 7 on gorse. This picture was taken five years after construction.

There are also rhododendron (middle right), brambles (middle bottom) and non-native conifers at the start of the access track, all of which will use the disturbed ground to work their way up the glen.

A bramble plant that has colonised the track about one kilometre up from the start, most likely spread by birds. Brambles are otherwise absent from this moorland.

Rushes which have colonised the disturbed ground.

The existing native trees are restricted to the riverside where the slopes are steeper and the soil drier. These woods have an unbroken link to when trees first colonised the locality thousands of years ago, and will be regenerating occasionally.

The area around the dam has been deer-fenced and Scots pine have been planted on the moorland. The planting has broken the long-term ecological continuity of the landscape, converting a wild one into a designed landscape.

The trees are likely to cause the demise of a plant rare or absent elsewhere in Scotland, the cyanobacterium (blue-green alga) *Gloeocapsa magma*, which has been called 'mountain dulse'. It is characteristic of this part of Wester Ross.

Peatland restoration

The latest intervention in the hills is that of peatland restoration – the return of peat bogs to a pristine state so that they can do their job of continuing to store carbon. This is why diggers can be encountered high up in the hills smoothing off vertical edges of exposed peat and filling-in or damming the erosion gullies. This is to 're-wet' the bog surface to allow the peat to start growing again and to prevent the exposed peat oxidising away and releasing its stored carbon into the air. There is plenty of government money to pay for this, as the need to restore peat bogs has become a mantra of 'nature-based solutions to global warming'. Whether the ancient blanket peats can ever be restored such that they restart sequestering carbon is questionable, although covering up exposed peat will certainly reduce the rate of carbon loss. Turning gullies into pools might slow down the erosion of the peat, but natural pools on peat are themselves erosion features, expanding in size over time.

The carbon benefits of this work could well be minimal overall, especially when the energy cost of taking mechanical diggers high into the hills and the increased methane output likely from the rewetted bogs are taken into account. The whole process is another example of human intervention in naturally wild landscapes.

The above refers to the 'restoration' of bogs, which on the whole are in a natural erosive phase of their lives. Where peatland restoration is of undoubted benefit is where human damage is being rectified, in particular the filling-in or damming of drainage ditches, or moor grips, which were widely ploughed through peat bogs for agricultural improvement, even in remote locations. They did not achieve their aim because blanket peat cannot be drained by digging ditches through it: water is held fast in the peat and cannot drain out, and some of the ditches have gone on to become erosion gullies.

Peatland restoration is also beneficial when it involves the removal of forestry plantations, because the tree roots dry out and oxidise the stored carbon. Planted bogs would have been forestry ploughed so this restoration includes the filling-in or damming of the plough-line hollows. In the past there was government money available to put in these forests, now there is money to remove them; and it is the same with the moor grips.

Felling of a forestry plantation by the RSPB on peatland in the Flow Country to stop the tree roots from drying out the peat and releasing the soil carbon.

Drainage ditches have been dug in peat across the Highlands. The aim was to dry the soil to provide better grazing for sheep. But water does not drain out of peat so the ditches never achieved their aim and are now being dammed or filled in to aid the climate.

A natural peat hagg on blanket peat showing exposed peat that will be oxidising to the air and releasing its stored carbon. There are now many projects to infill or dam these natural gullies, and to re-profile any vertical edges of peat.

Commercial forestry being removed from a raised bog, the Mòine Mhòr in Argyll. Unplanted peatland is visible in the background.

A moden scheme to restore blanket peat. Gullies are dammed and areas of exposed peat revegetated. It may be difficult to restart peat growth in ancient bogs such as these.

Diggers are now increasingly seen on peatlands, even at relatively high altitudes, to carry out restoration work. 'Restoration' of naturally eroding bogs may help the climate to some extent but will reduce the overall naturalness or wildness of peatlands.

A natural gully blocked with a wood/peat dam, creating pools. The water table will be raised on the sides of the gully ('rewetting'). Peat oxidation/erosion is still likely to continue underwater so the long-term impact is unclear.

The accumulation of small structures

There are many small-scale intrusions into the Highland landscape in addition to the interventions discussed already.

Shieling sites date back hundreds of years and the remains of the small huts can still be seen, as can occasional huts or bothies dating from sheep farming days. There are also some older archaeological remains such as hut circles and more recent ones such as fanks for sheep farming and coastal structures associated with the Second World War. In the 1800s the Ordnance Survey began mapping the Highlands and constructed huts at high altitude near the main triangulation stations (Colby Camps), the remains of which are still visible in some places. Small triangulation pillars (trig points) on the summits are a sight common to any hillwalker.

Landowners sometimes take diggers into the hills to restructure burns and rivers to improve fishing, resulting in canalisation, the deepening of pools and obvious spoil heaps. Reinforcement of eroding track sides, riverbanks and coasts can involve the use of rock armouring – often using rock imported from elsewhere which is positioned unnaturally – and gabions (wire cages filled with rock). These modern structures fit into the landscape less well than traditional stone walls built with native rock.

Grouse shooting estates can create lines of shooting butts and dig pools for grouse. Other structures include cairns, signposts, notice boards, feeding troughs for livestock, footbridges and fish cages in lochs. Litter adds a human dimension to the landscape, particularly along the coast.

Stone removal and the deepening of the natural pools of a burn on the Island of Jura to improve the fishing.

An old fank in Wester Ross used for gathering sheep.

A trig point built by Ordnance Survey to aid mapping. These are a common sight on hill tops, although they are no longer required by Ordnance Survey.

A pool created by a digger on a grouse moor in the Monadhliath Mountains, to provide more insects for grouse to eat.

Footbridges enable easy access to areas otherwise hard to reach. The same applies to road bridges: before these were built it was hard to travel across the Highlands.

Fish cages in Loch Awe, a common sight in many freshwater lochs. These result in no permanent landscape change as they are easily removable, although sometimes there is an associated permanent track, jetty or building.

Rock-filled wire baskets or gabions, constructed to prevent erosion along the side of a hill track. It cannot be said that such gabions are things of beauty, unlike the traditional stone retaining walls that would have been built in such places in the past.

Invasive and introduced plants

One of the commonest invasive plants entering many parts of the Highlands is gorse, a thorny shrub traditionally known in Scotland as whin. Osgood Mackenzie in early 1900 found gorse seeds at the bottom of peat bogs in Wester Ross, which an expert identified as likely to be those of gorse or possibly broom. He says:[13]

> East Coast gentlemen will perhaps be astonished to hear that neither the whin or the broom are native plants here. One hundred years ago, the only broom plants in the district were a few sown round the garden of my far back predecessors in this place, and the first whins that ever grew anywhere near here were produced from seed sown by a minister on the Poolewe glebe, and some sown also by a member of the Letterewe family at Udrigal. It is certain it was not an indigenous plant here in modern times, whatever it might have been [in the distant past].

Gorse was also introduced to Sutherland and has never been native to the Long Island, Orkney, Shetland, Coll or Tiree. It is a highly invasive plant in New Zealand and other countries. In the Highlands, roadsides provide a major route for its colonisation into new areas and most roads now have a string of gorse bushes alongside them, including the 15-mile stretch from Drumrunie to Achiltibuie in Wester Ross. Road construction and improvements disturb the soil, providing an excellent seedbed for gorses and many other plants and trees. Once there is a strong population along the roads the large seed rain produced means that the plants often seed out into the wider landscape.

For many miles on Highland roads the views are obscured by roadside trees. In some cases these are trees planted during improvements but often they are native trees or commercial conifers which have colonised the ideal growing conditions of the disturbed ground, sometimes assisted by roadside fencing which reduces grazing pressure. Soil disturbance helps non-native plants gain a foothold, whether garden escapes or self-seeding trees from plantations. Without action, the whole landscape of the Highlands will be transformed over the next hundred years or so by these new species.

Perhaps the greatest transformation could be brought about by the exponential expansion of Sitka spruce seeding-out from commercial plantations; it was chosen to be the dominant forestry tree because it is well suited to the Scottish soils and climate. It may not grow as vigorously on unploughed land, but survives in places with undisturbed soil and is eclectic in where it grows – whether open moor, crags, peat bogs or native woods. Its spiky needles give it greater resistance to grazing than Scotland's native trees. It is native only to North America but had it been indigenous to Scotland the Highland landscape is likely to have become something very different, with forest still common. The spruce is more suited to the Highlands than our own native trees! See Case Study 2 on p. 97.

Other non-native conifers also seed out into the wider countryside, such as lodgepole pine, Lawson's cypress and larches. One species of rhododendron has the potential

American skunk cabbage colonising a shoreline on Mull. Note the colonising Sitka spruce and gorse in the background.

to transform the landscape on a large scale – *Rhododendron ponticum*. The success of this plant is partly down to Victorian horticulturalists who selected hardy varieties and inserted foreign genes through cross-breeding. The location of the 'big house' in any Highland glen is easily recognised by being at the centre of a spreading infection of rhododendron (see photograph on p. 78).

Like the Sitka spruce it happily grows anywhere in the wetter western half of the Highlands, whether open moor, hillside, woodland or bog. Unlike Sitka spruce, however, which dies when cut down, rhododendron is hard to eradicate. Much better to control it before it becomes too common in a particular locality.

There are many other plants from different parts of the world taking over the Highlands. Some are inconspicuous albeit ubiquitous, such as New Zealand willowherb and the moss *Campylopus introflexus*, but others are likely to become increasingly obvious over time. Among them are the Japanese knotweed and Himalayan balsam along coasts and riversides; the skunk cabbage from North America in damp areas and along watercourses; various species of *Cotoneaster*, which can take over whole cliffs such as that below Dunvegan Castle on Skye and which are hard to control because their berries are spread by birds; the distinctive orange-flowered montbretia, which is escaping outwards from settlements in the west; *Mimulus* or monkeyflower in ditches in the Western Isles; the two large species of *Gunnera* from Brazil; and one shrub that is a huge problem in New Zealand and soon will be here, the Himalayan honeysuckle *Leycesteria formosa*, also known as flowering nutmeg. This plant is already taking over the hillside above the road between Nether Lochaber and Fort William and is spreading out from gardens all over. There are others, including lesser knotweed, *Gaultheria*, *Acaena* and *Buddleia*.

A Highland landscape dominated by self-seeded Sitka spruce, rhododendron, cotoneaster, swamp cabbage and Himalayan honeysuckle will be very different from that we know today, but, surprisingly, little notice is being taken. People are far too busy doing visionary things such as planting new woods or restoring peat bogs.

153

Gorse *Ulex europaeus*, which has colonised the originally heather-dominated Drummossie Muir south of Inverness. See also Case Study 7 on gorse.

Early-stage colonisation of wet moorland by rhododendron and Sitka spruce in Gairloch, Wester Ross. See also Case Studies 2 and 8.

Himalayan honeysuckle *Leycesteria formosa*, a plant commonly planted in gardens and now escaping across the country.

A hillslope on clear-felled forestry land above the A82 trunk road between Nether Lochaber and Fort William now colonised by *Leycesteria*, the plant dominating the vegetation. This species can spread very quickly.

Japanese knotweed (left), Himalayan balsam *Impatiens glandulifera* (right) and the osier *Salix viminalis* (background) colonising shingle banks along the River Spey near its mouth. None of these species are native to the British Isles.

A modern Highland landscape on Mull, dominated by Sitka spruce and skunk cabbage, both originally from North America.

Gaultheria (*Pernettya*) has escaped from a garden and is now invading a pine plantation. It is from southern South America and If uncontrolled can become the dominant understorey.

Birds eat the purple berries of *Gaultheria* and hence spread it; it is the same with the red-berried *Cotoneaster* species below.

A *Cotoneaster* species (dark green) which has escaped from a nearby garden and now smothers a cliff in Argyll. It is colonising cliffs and slopes on Mull to the detriment of native plants and animals.

A *Cotoneaster* species (brown) which has colonised the cliff below Dunvegan Castle on the Isle of Skye.

Another species of *Cotoneaster* in Plockton. The vegetation of many Highland villages where there is no grazing is increasingly becoming a mix of garden escapees, including *Cotoneaster*, *Buddleia*, *Leycesteria*, *Rhododendron ponticum*, Japanese knotweed and montbretia. Brambles and gorse are often common as well.

Two species of the large-leaved *Gunnera* from Brazil are widely planted in gardens. Here the *Gunnera* is colonising a location in Argyll. The plant is also problematic on peat bogs in the west of Ireland.

CASE STUDY 7

The spread of gorse (Ulex europeaus)

Roadsides are major corridors for introducing gorse to new areas, here the road down to Gruinard Bay in Wester Ross. The disturbed ground from road construction and road improvements provides an excellent seedbed for gorse and other plants to colonise. The slipstream from vehicles may well aid the movement of gorse seeds along the road.

The complete takeover of heather moorland by gorse, here part of Drummossie Muir south of Inverness.

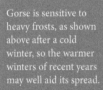

Gorse is sensitive to heavy frosts, as shown above after a cold winter, so the warmer winters of recent years may well aid its spread.

A forestry track acting as a conduit for the spread of gorse.

A footpath in Wester Ross through an area of moorland now colonised by gorse.

Gorse spreading up a dry hillslope above Gairloch in Wester Ross.

Gorse invading moorland south of Inverness.

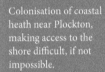

Colonisation of coastal heath near Plockton, making access to the shore difficult, if not impossible.

The first plant of gorse colonising the disturbed ground along the edge of a new track to a hydro-electric scheme in Wester Ross (the same location as Case Study 6). The presence of this track will allow the plant to spread up a glen where it is not currently present.

CASE STUDY 8
The spread of Rhododendron ponticum

Rhododendron taking over a moorland landscape on the island of Islay. Note the young rhododendron colonising the vegetation in the foreground. Removal of early colonists will prevent the need for the difficult and time-consuming business of removing an established stand. Unlike Sitka spruce, the plant is not killed by cutting: cut shoots regenerate from the stump so that in most cases chemical treatment is needed to eradicate the plant.

Another example of rhododendron takeover on Islay. Note the electricity pole centre right for scale.

Rhododendron now dominating the slopes of the Great Glen above Letterfinlay.

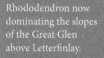

Colonising a peat bog on the island of Raasay. Note also the Sitka spruce plantation in the background, illustrating how many landscapes are being transformed into a modern rhododendron–Sitka type.

Early stage of colonisation of moorland above Loch Torridon in Wester Ross. A rhododendron eradication programme has recently taken place in this area, an expensive and long-term process, because there has to be follow-up control for many years.

A modern Highland landscape in Argyll of self-seeded conifers and rhododendron with its distinctive purple flowers.

The plant has spread from the 'big house', in this case Duncraig Castle near Plockton, to dominate both open ground and the surrounding woodland.

A path through a dense stand of rhododendron on the island of Arran. This shows how the plant takes over the landscape, allowing nothing else to grow.

A dense stand on the island of Arran on land owned by the National Trust for Scotland, which has been cleared. Regenerating shoots are visible from the stumps, which have to be treated with chemicals to totally kill the plant.

Chapter 5

Lamentation or celebration?

Imagination and reality

There are the Highlands of the imagination, a land of hills and moors, lochs and rivers, coasts and islands, all untrammelled, still pure in the mind. Some of the mountains are craggy and overbearing, others more homely, rounded and smooth, albeit wild during a snow-blasted blizzard or in endless mist and rain. The moors are wide open, windswept, heather clad. There is room to breathe and space to live. A golden eagle might soar above; an antlered stag may be outlined against a clear horizon. The woods are of wide-crowned, blue-tinged pine trees set apart by heather, the trunks a golden orange in the evening sun. The long, straight, wave-covered lochs are trapped between the hills, but some, snake-like, wind their way into the sea. Our rivers, likewise, wind in long meanders to the coast, their tributaries tumbling over rocks and falls, in a hurry to join them, bringing white scars to the hillsides in times of spate. We have the glories of a sunset over an island-studded sea, the sun setting in the west and, behind, the starkly-edged, gold-rimmed cloud wrack heralding another storm. In the evening, there is the

The Allt a' Gharbhrain below Beinn Dearg, Wester Ross.

coming home to a heart-warming peat fire after a long walk during a short winter's day, with a ceilidh of song, dance and drink to round things off.

This is the Highlands of the tourist brochure, a landscape where nature is still in charge, that has escaped the trappings and ravages of the modern world – one likely to remain strong in the imagination of the exiled Highlander. It is also the landscape beloved of film-makers in their historical dramas, providing a romantic backdrop to the events portrayed. But keen-eyed observers know that in such films it is hard to avoid the occasional anachronism of a Sitka spruce plantation in an era way before the tree was introduced to Scotland, or a track in what would then have been a trackless land. This is because unspoilt land – land unsullied by modern intrusions and where nature still rules – is now hard to find in the real Highlands.

Instead are pylons and poles traversing the landscape, masts and wind turbines atop many hills, and bulldozed tracks up the glens. Many hills and moors are a mosaic of burnt vegetation, lochs are now reservoirs with dams and ugly drawdown zones,

A lochan below Beinn Chapull, Argyll.

Coire Gabhail or The Lost Valley, Glencoe.

Sgùrr nan Gillean from Sligachan, Isle of Skye (The Black Cuillin).

and there are fences and plantations for miles, the scars of forestry ploughing and the pervasive rhododendron and Sitka spruce.

Why do the people of Scotland allow this to happen? Why no clamour to slow landscape change or keep some areas wild? Accusations were made earlier that outsiders have forever been coming to the Highlands and telling the Highlander what to do. But for those brought up and living in a region the sheer familiarity leads to a lack of objectivity. Even those who settle in an area because of its scenic beauty, find after a few years that they are taking the beauty for granted. It is exiled Highlanders who retain the image of the landscape in their minds and who, when returning, see the land with more objective eyes – in the same way that an observant tourist might.

This may help explain why Highland folk tend to let the changes of the modern world sweep over the land. In the Highlands in particular, with its history of depopulation and generally low wages, the priority has always been the provision of jobs and investment. Economic development is always more important, but one day, once the golden age of economic prosperity for all has arrived, perhaps we can think about side issues such as the landscape. Meanwhile the tourist brochures carry on as if nothing is happening –

Meall Odhar above Loch Loyne, Inverness-shire.

In Glen Buidhe, above Loch Creran, Argyll.

Above Trinafour, Perthshire.

Above Glen Fyne, Argyll.

'Come to the wild Highlands' – even if it is wild no longer. In this respect, the Highlands are little different from many rural areas across the world. But the end result is nature in full retreat. Even where there is action to restore nature, some, such as the expansion of tree cover, is having the opposite effect – albeit carried out with good intent.

Do all these changes to the landscape really matter? Should we just accept them or instead let emotion take over and sing a lament, so beloved of the Gael, for the loss of the authentic land of hill and moor? For unless emotion takes over, nothing will change.

But emotion will not be enough to save it, so we must turn to practicalities. Land has to be sacrificed to satisfy our modern needs, but much is to be gained by better looking after the remaining fragments of authentic Highland landscape, not in economic terms but in the knowledge that there is still a little corner of the Earth beyond our control, a corner our ancestors would have known so well.

This is not an easy thing to do because the land is not ours to do with as we will because there is little history of state-owned land in Scotland. And landowners, whether private or community, see it as their inalienable right to be able to make money from the land. This right is so built into our culture that if an owner is requested by society not to do something, compensation for 'profits foregone' is demanded. And it is certainly not fair that, if a local community has finally managed to acquire a parcel of the Highlands, they are then not allowed to make use of it. There are some rich landowners who do not need the land to earn an income, but those managing their land often aim to maximise income by seeking government grants.

Most large-scale changes to the landscape of the Highlands, and most of rural Britain, are brought about by such grants – they are paid for by you and me through taxation or bills. Forest and woodland creation and agriculture is grant-aided, renewable energy developers have government incentives, peatland restoration is currently having money thrown at it. Only estates managed for deer stalking or grouse shooting are not dependent on government subsidies. Thus, many changes could be stopped if government incentives were removed, either throughout the Highlands or only in certain locations. But this will only happen if society demands it, and there is no sign of this at present – the opposite is the case. It is likely that the landscape will continue to evolve in an ad hoc manner dependent on the uptake of government grants, and continue to be fragmented in an almost random way.

The formal approach

Yet the landscape of the Highlands has always been seen as something special. At the end of the Second World War, almost as a thank you to the people for the sacrifices they had made, the Ramsay Committee recommended five National Parks for the Highlands,[1] although it took over fifty years to get the two we have – The Cairngorms, and Loch Lomond and the Trossachs. But by law these two must reconcile conservation with economic development, making it difficult to give priority to the landscape.

The five areas originally suggested as National Parks were recognised in planning circles as National Park Direction Areas for many years. These only ceased to exist when Scotland's national landscape designation, National Scenic Areas, came into being in 1981.[2] There are forty of these, most of them in the Highlands, designed to represent the best of Scotland's iconic scenery. Each has had its 'special qualities' identified, which, added together, give each its iconic status. In theory this should make it easy to identify whether or not a proposed development will fit into the landscape. But the language of landscape, unlike that of nature conservation, tends to be woolly and imprecise.[3] For example, the special qualities of the Assynt-Coigach National Scenic Area include "Spectacular scenery of lone mountains", "Settlements nestled within a wider landscape of mountain peaks, wild moorlands, and rocky seascapes", "A landscape of vast open space and exposure" and "Unexpected and extensive tracts of native woodland". This imprecision makes it relatively easy for developers to work round the special landscape features and achieve what they want. And the tree planters are so obsessed that they rarely stop to look at the special qualities before planting their trees, even if one stated quality is "Great expanses of open moorland".

For reasons that are unclear, National Scenic Areas have had little resonance with the people of Scotland: perhaps the term Area of Outstanding Natural Beauty, the one used

East of Loch Awe, Argyll.

in the rest of the United Kingdom, would have more resonance. As it is, it is probably true that most people, even if they have heard of them, would be hard put to say where they are or what they mean in practice. Where the designations of National Park and National Scenic Area have had impact is in preventing windfarms being sited within them.

There are other smaller-scale designations determined by local authorities, although again few people probably realise this. National Scenic Areas and local designations are taken into account by planners in local planning decisions, but forestry and agriculture fall outwith the planning system. However, the pressure for development is such that most developers get their way.

A more recent designation developed by the government agency NatureScot (previously Scottish Natural Heritage) is that of a Wild Land Area, of which there are forty-two, mostly in the Highlands.[4] These were identified on the basis of research which studied the whole of Scotland and thereafter mapped the wildest areas – land without, or with a minimum, of infrastructure, although in this case 'infrastructure' excludes woodland plantations and the associated fences. Government guidance to developers and planners indicates a presumption against new development in these – with the exception of new renewable energy infrastructure, which is to be allowed.[5] The result will be that wildness continues to decline. Often wild land gets a bad press in the Highlands because it is erroneously believed that all of it was once peopled and should now be repopulated: development, it is argued, in such areas is therefore appropriate.

None of these different designations, National Park, National Scenic Area, Wild Land Area and local designations, have strong legal backing and might be more accurately termed 'labels': they merely highlight important landscapes rather than providing strong protection. In addition, some nature conservation designations, particularly Special Areas of Conservation for habitats and Special Protection Areas[6] for

Glen Damff, Angus.

birds can be de facto landscape designations: if an area is designated for open moorland, or for golden eagles, this may mean that the landscape is kept free of trees. It is unclear, though, how strong these European designations will remain now that Britain has left the European Union.

There is also an informal designation that applies to the upland properties owned by the National Trust for Scotland, the 'Unna properties', where the 'Unna Principles' apply. Percy Unna was chairman of the Scottish Mountaineering Club in the 1930s and raised money from club members and other British mountaineering clubs to buy the estate of Glencoe and Dalness so that it could be gifted to the National Trust for Scotland. This was on the understanding that certain principles would be accepted, the main being:

> To undertake that the land be maintained in its primitive condition for all time with unrestricted
> access to the public ... that 'primitive' means not less primitive that the existing state.

Nowadays we would use the term 'wild land' instead of 'primitive'. Other Unna Principles include: the mountains should not be made safer to climb; mechanical transport should not be used; no new paths should be constructed or improved; no signposts or waymarks should be erected; no shelters should be built in the hills; and there should be no deer stalking.[7] The Trust has had to accept modifications – many

Looking towards Beinn Ghlas from Ben Cruachan, Argyll.

upland paths have to be improved to prevent them washing away and causing erosion scars, and the Trust does carry out deer stalking as part of its habitat management programme. The money raised by Unna also enabled the Trust to buy the properties Ben Lawers, Torridon, Kintail and Goatfell where the Unna Principles apply.

But there does not seem to be any strong will, whether from government, local authorities or the public, to give stronger protection to the Highland landscape, which is why it continues to disappear. Only when there is strong pressure on politicians from the public is anything likely to change in this regard; currently the development lobby appears to have the upper hand. What happened to the post-war enthusiasm that first suggested National Parks?

Most people do not realise how quickly the landscape has changed and is still changing. The presence of trees everywhere is a recent phenomenon as is clear from photographs from around 1900. A wooded landscape is now the new normal in many areas – in Strathspey, for example. In numerous places so many trees have been put into the landscape that it is possible that an ecological tipping point has been reached: the seed rain from trees on any remaining open ground is so large that any return to open landscape might be impossible. Indeed, many of the changes discussed in Chapter 4 are irreversible. This makes it even more important to protect what is still left of the traditional Highland landscape – if this is still possible.

The other country: a new future?

This book has told of one country, the country of change we have today. But there's another country – perhaps an imaginary one, or an ideal. It could exist, for glimpses can be seen if you clamber over the fence, beyond the wall of trees, behind the rotating turbines, on the far side of the electrified loch, out of the reach of the farthest track. A country where the hills are real and untarnished, the moors untamed, the peatlands untouched, where the burns find their own way to the sea, where the rivers and riversides decide for themselves how they want to be, where the lochs are undammed, the coastline undeveloped, the deer wild and free – a country left to itself. It is still there, hanging on, but it is encircled and, as a stoat traps a rabbit, the circle is becoming smaller every year.

But is it possible for this ancient Scotland to survive the modern era? It can certainly be imagined: a country where wild land is celebrated within and outwith the Highlands; where wild areas are protected by statute, where no new infrastructure is allowed and there is no possibility of exemptions; where new bulldozed tracks are illegal and unneeded

Hills of the Cluanie Ridge, Inverness-shire.

tracks are removed; where no vehicles are permitted off the road to leave their wheel marks on the land and where there are no fences and where forestry grants are unavailable.

Where the only management allowed is low-intensity livestock grazing; where the harvesting of a natural surplus through low-impact red deer stalking or low-intensity grouse shooting is possible; where informal recreation enables us to appreciate these areas to the full, as long as there is money to keep the paths in good repair; and where there is reintroduction of species knowingly made extinct by humans and whose habitat is still naturally extant and likely to remain so – true rewilding; where the ground is not disturbed and the only other activities are the repair of the damage we have caused, such as the filling-in of ditches and removal of plantations from bogs.

Land where, perhaps most importantly, the energy currently devoted to planting trees is instead directed to the removal of invasive plants; where a Sitka spruce or other conifer straying beyond its plantation is removed at the plantation owner's expense – the polluter pays; where 'rewilding' no longer results in a loss of wildness but a full

Crossing the Highland watershed – the new: the A9 trunk road near Dalwhinnie.

Sheep farming: a land use compatible with maintaining the traditional Highland open landscape.

Cattle grazing: a land use also in tandem with maintaining the traditional Highland open landscape.

Crossing the Highland watershed – the old: the Fain or Destitution Road (A832).

Deer stalking: a land use compatible with maintaining the traditional Highland open landscape.

Low-intensity grouse shooting: a land use also compatible with maintaining the traditional Highland open landscape.

appreciation of the true wildness of the Highlands based on an understanding of its ecological history; where developers realise that it is just as much their land as our land, they and their descendants having to live with the consequences; where tourism businesses are defenders of the asset that brings tourists in the first place; where owners and communities do not have to extract every last penny of income from their holdings but are compensated for allowing their land to be wild; where accounting, targets and outcomes are relegated to the bin and bandwagons run into the sand. Not impossible, surely, for is this not what Percy Unna envisaged when donating Glencoe to the National Trust for Scotland?

But what of the areas that have not been formally identified as wild? Is this wildness to be lost because we always need at least some development? If we must sacrifice some areas for the greater good we must be sensitive in our action, and always leave some space for the untamed.

To quote again Lord Cockburn when standing at the top of the Rest and Be Thankful in 1838:

> As I stood at the height of the road and gazed down on its strange course both ways, I could not help rejoicing that there was at least one place where railways, canals, and steamers and all these devices for sinking hills and raising valleys, and introducing man and levels, and destroying solitude and nature, would for ever be set at defiance.

His 'for ever' has been short-lived, for the eastern approach to the pass is now an industrial forestry plantation and a heavily engineered trunk road. The top of the pass is a car park with a phone mast and the western approach rises from plantations through a glen slowly being colonised by self-seeded Sitka spruce. The hand of humankind is everywhere, and solitude impossible because of the road; nature is in full retreat. Was Lord Cockburn too much of an idealist? Can this 'other country' ever exist and, if so, is it not in our hands to create? Surely we do not want to leave our world impoverished, a land where nature in the raw can no longer be enjoyed, where we remain forever trapped in our own civilisation, with no possibility for escape?

Notes and references

Chapter 1

1   'Woolly maggots', a term used by George Monbiot in 2013. See https://www.monbiot.com/2013/05/30/sheepwrecked/

2   In *West Highland Survey: An Essay in Human Ecology*, p. 192, edited by Frank Fraser Darling. Published in 1955 by Oxford University Press.

3   In *On the Other Side of Sorrow: Nature and People in the Scottish Highlands*, p. 149, by James Hunter, published in 1995 by Mainstream Publishing, Edinburgh and London. A whole chapter of this book is called 'The Highlands are a Devastated Countryside'.

4   In *Regeneration: The Rescue of a Wild Land* by Andrew Painting, p. 10. Published in 2021 by Birlinn, Edinburgh.

5   From the *Perthshire Advertiser*, 28 December 1960, after a walk by Ian MacArthur MP through Glen Affric, and quoted in *The Dam Builders* by James Miller, p. 225, published in 2002 by Birlinn.

6   In *A Naturalist in the Highlands 1767–1771*, by James Robertson, edited by D.M. Henderson and J.H. Dickson. Published in 1994 by Scottish Academic Press.

7   From *The Drove Roads of Scotland*, by A.R.B. Haldane, p. 210. First published in 1952 by Thomas Nelson and Sons.

8   Heather moorland and peat bogs have been recognised in Annex 1 of the 1992 EC Habitats Directive: see https://ec.europa.eu/environment/nature/legislation/habitatsdirective/index_en.htm

9   In *On the Other Side of Sorrow: Nature and People in the Scottish Highlands*, by James Hunter. See note ch1, 3.

10 Published in *Poems of the Scottish Hills*, an anthology selected by Hamish Brown and published by Aberdeen University Press in 1982.

11 From 'Braemar down Glenshee to Perth', 1853, in *Circuit Journeys*, by Lord Cockburn. Published in 1983 by Byways Books, Hawick.

12 The political nature of grouse moor management is illustrated in Ian Coghill's book *Moorland Matters,* published by Quiller in 2021 and which, although largely referring to English moors, has some applicability to Highland moors.

Chapter 2

1   The Rough Bounds is another name for Knoydart.

2   The Long Island is another name for the chain of islands making up The Outer Hebrides.

3   An old evocative name used by farmers for purple moor grass, *Molinia caerulea*, owing to the tendency for its profusion of dead leaves to fly about in the wind.

4   Here referring to Sibelius' tone poem *Tapiola*.

5   From 'The Song of the Open Road' in The Rime of True Thomas by John Buchan.

6   'At the Rest and Be Thankful,' 1838, in *Circuit Journeys* by Lord Cockburn. See note ch1, 11.

7   'Through Glen Moriston, past Loch Cluny and down Glen Shiel,' 1841, in *Circuit Journeys* by Lord Cockburn. See note ch1, 11.

8   Translated from the Gaelic by Robert Buchanan. Note the word "forest" is here used in the old meaning of uncultivated land, such as in the "deer forest" of today.

9   Translated from the Gaelic by Marjory Kennedy-Fraser.

10 The Roy maps are available to view on the National Library of Scotland's website https://maps.nls.uk/roy/.

11 From *An Illustrated Guide to British Upland Vegetation* by A. Averis et al., p. 15. Published in 2004 by the Joint Nature Conservation Committee, Peterborough.

12 As described in *From an Antique Land: Visual representations of the Highlands and Islands 1700–1880* by Anne Macleod. Published in 2012 by John Donald, Edinburgh.

13 From a paper by O.H. Mackenzie given to the Inverness Field Club, quoted in the section 'Peat Bogs' in Alexander Polson's *Gairloch and Wester Ross*, published c.1907 by George Souter, Dingwall.

14 From 'Late-Quaternary Biotic Changes in Terrestrial and Lacustrine Environments, with Particular Reference to North-west Europe', by H.J.B. Birks, pp. 3–65, 1986. In: B.E. Berglund (editor) *Handbook of Holocene Palaeoecology and Palaeohydrology*.

15 See 'The Rise and Fall of Forests', 2004, by J. Birks and H. Birks. In *Science*, Volume 305, Issue 5, 683, pp. 484–5.

16   See *An Illustrated Book of Peat. The life and death of bogs: A new synthesis*, 2021, by James H.C. Fenton for more discussion of how peat forms and expands to cover the landscape. The book is available from https://www.nhbs.com.

17   From 'On the buried forests and peat mosses of Scotland, and the changes of climate which they indicate', 1867 (read in 1866), by James Geikie. In *Transactions of the Royal Society, Edinburgh*, Vol. XXIV, Part II, pp. 363–384.

18   From *The Holocene history of* Pinus sylvestris *woodland in the Mar Lodge Estate, Cairngorms, Eastern Scotland* by Danny Paterson. PhD thesis submitted to the University of Stirling, 2011.

19   From *Loch Maree* by H.J.B. Birks. In 'Geological Conservation Review' 1988–2007, Joint Nature Conservation Committee, Peterborough.

20   From '"Natural" vegetation in Britain: the pollen-eye view', 2018, by R. Fyfe. In *British Wildlife*, Volume 25, pp. 339–349.

21   See Chapter 2 'Woods of Imagination and Reality' in the book *Nature Contested* by T.C. Smout. Published in 2000 by Edinburgh University Press.

22   See *The Highland House Transformed: Architecture and Identity on the Edge of Britain 1700–1850*, by Maudlin Daniel. Published in 2009 by Edinburgh University Press.

23   From 'A review of natural vegetation openness in north-western Europe', 2002, by J-C. Svenning. In *Biological Conservation*, Volume 104, pp. 133–148.

24   See *Grazing Ecology and Forest History* by Frans Vera. Published in 2000 by CABI Publishing, Wallingford.

25   This whole topic is discussed in more detail in 'A postulated natural origin for the open landscape of upland Scotland', 2008, by James H.C. Fenton. In *Plant Ecology and Diversity*, Volume 1, pp. 115–127.

26   *The History of British Mammals* by Derek Yalden. Published in 1999 by T. & A. D. Poyser, London.

27   From *A Highland Deer Herd and its Management: A study of the red deer population and its impact on the habitat of the Letterewe Estate, Wester Ross*, by Jos Milner, Jim Alexander and Cy Griffin, p. 31. Published in 2002 by Red Lion House, London.

28   See note ch2, 10.

29   Ian Macleod, quoted in *The Herald*, 5 February 2014, p. 10.

30   Kaplan, quoted in *New Scientist*, 16 November 2013, p. 37.

31   See *An Illustrated Book of Peat. The life and death of bogs: A new synthesis*, 2021, by James H.C. Fenton. See note ch2, 16.

32   Ibid.

33   Ibid.

34   As discussed in *Heathland*, by Clive Chatters. Published in 2021 by Bloomsbury Wildlife, London.

35   Ibid.

36   From *The Scottish Clearances: A History of the Dispossessed*, by Tom Devine, p. 19. Published in 2018 by Penguin Random House (Allen Lane).

37   From *The Drove Roads of Scotland*, p. 210. See note ch1, 7.

38   Ibid.

39   From The Demise of Scotland's Woodlands from c. 4000 CAL BC to c. AD1000, by Richard Tipping. In *Scottish Woodland History Conference, Notes XX, Tracing the decline of the "Caledonian Forest" over six millennia*, 2015, edited by Mairi Stewart.

40   From *The Northern Isles: Orkney and Shetland*, by Alexander Fenton. 1997 edition published by the Tuckworth Press, East Linton.

41   Ibid.

42   The European Landscape Convention is an initiative of the Council of Europe, not the European Union.

43   See *The Experience of Landscape* by Jay Appleton. Published in 1995 by John Wiley and Sons.

44   *The History of British Mammals* by Yalden. See note ch2, 26.

45   As mentioned in *The Finest Road in the World*, p. 154, by James Miller. Published in 2017 by Birlinn.

Chapter 3

1   Ploughing releases the carbon stored in the soil to the air through drying and oxidation.

2   Forest and Land Scotland, previously the Scottish arm of the Forestry Commission.

3   From 'On the buried forests and peat mosses of Scotland, and the changes of climate which they indicate', by James Geikie. See note ch2, 17.

4   From 'The great myth of Caledon', 1992, by David Breeze. In *Scottish Forestry*. Volume 46, pp. 331–335.

5   The opening sentence of the chapter 'Woods of Imagination and Reality' in *Nature Contested: Environmental History in Scotland and Northern Island* by T.C. Smout. See note ch2, 21.

6   See 'Studies of Scottish moorland in relation to tree growth' by G.K. Fraser in *Bulletin of the Forestry Commission, No.15*, HMSO, Edinburgh.

7   Cairngorms Connect is a partnership of organisations: see https://cairngormsconnect.org.uk/

8   From 'Taylor, The Water Poet' in *Early Travellers in Scotland*, edited by Peter Hume Brown. Facsimile of 1891 edition, published by James Thin, Edinburgh in 1973.

9   From *A Naturalist in the Highlands 1767–1771*, p. 154. See note ch1, 6.

10 In 'The Ecology and Restoration of Montane and Subalpine Scrub Habitats in Scotland', 1997, edited by M.E.D. Poore. *Scottish Natural Heritage Review No. 83*, pp. 115–116.

11 See for example, *The Little Ice Age: How climate made history 1300–1850*, by Brian Fagan. Published in 2002 by Basic Books.

12 See for example, 'Developing guidance for managing extensive upland grazing where habitats have differing requirements', 2010, by J.P. Holland, et al., *Scottish Natural Heritage Commissioned Report No. 402*.

13 In *Heathland*, by Clive Chatters. See note ch2, 34.

14 See *The Scottish Clearances: A History of the Dispossessed* by Tom Devine. See note ch2, 36.

15 See note ch2, 10.

16 From *A Naturalist in the Highlands 1767–1771*, p. 161. See note ch1, 6.

17 From 'Grasslands of the Forest and Sub-alpine Zones' by J. King and I.A. Nicholson, pp. 168–231. In: J.H. Burnett (editor) *The Vegetation of Scotland* published in 1964 by Oliver and Boyd, Edinburgh & London.

18 See, for example, *The State of Highland Birchwoods: The report of the Scottish Wildlife Trust 1984 survey of birchwoods in Highland Region*, by James Fenton. Available online at https://www.fenton.scot/scientific.htm

19 From 'Taylor, The Water Poet' in *Early Travellers in Scotland*. See note ch3, 8.

20 From *A Naturalist in the Highlands 1767–1771*, p. 167. See note ch1, 6.

21 From *Description of the Occidental Islands of Scotland*, by Donald Monro, c.1549. Published together with Martin Martin's book of 1695. See note ch3, 22.

22 From *A Description of the Western Islands of Scotland* by Martin Martin, c.1695. Published in 1999 by Birlinn.

23 From *A Naturalist in the Highlands 1767–1771*, p. 88. See note ch1, 6.

24 As discussed in 'The role of grazing in maintain open landscapes in temperate regions', by James Fenton, published in *The International Journal of Environmental Sciences and Natural Resources*, January 2023, 17 pages.

25 See 'Exploring a natural baseline for large-herbivore biomass in ecological restoration', by C. Fløjgaard, et al.. Published in the *Journal of Applied Ecology*, November 2021.

26 *Rewilding*, by Paul Jepson and Cain Blythe (illustrated edition), published by Icon Books, London, 2021.

27 As discussed in 'The role of grazing in maintaining open landscapes in temperate regions' by James Fenton. See note ch3, 24.

28 See, for example, 'What if wolves don't change rivers, or the lynx lacks bite? Rethinking a rewilding orthodoxy', 2021, by Hugh Webster. In *British Wildlife*, Volume 33, pp. 91–98.

29 'Red deer grazing on Pirbright Ranges', 2021, by RSPB. In *British Wildlife*, Volume 21, pp. 98–99.

30 See 'Global response of fire activity to late Quaternary grazer extinctions', 2021, by A.T. Karp, et al., published in *Science*, Vol 374, Issue 6,571, pp. 1145–1148.

31 From *The Demise of Scotland's Woodlands from c. 4000 BC to c. 1000 AD* by Richard Tipping. See note ch2, 39.

32 From 'Taylor, The Water Poet' in *Early Travellers in Scotland*. See note ch3, 8.

33 Available to view on the National Library of Scotland website at https://maps.nls.uk/counties/rec/198

34 See *The Holocene history of* Pinus sylvestris *woodland in the Mar Lodge Estate, Cairngorms, Eastern Scotland* by Danny Paterson. See note ch2, 18.

35 From *Loch Maree* by H.J.B. Birks. See note ch2, 19.

36 From 'Charcoal iron smelting and its fuel supply: the example of Lorn Furnace, Argyllshire 1753–1876', 1975, by James Lindsay. In the *Journal of Historical Geography*, Volume 1, pp. 283–298, and quoted in T.C. Smout. See note ch2, 21.

37 In *Nature Contested*, p. 56, by T.C. Smout. See note ch2, 21.

38 See *An Illustrated Book of Peat. The life and death of bogs: A new synthesis, 2021*, by James H.C. Fenton. See note ch2, 16.

39 Ibid.

40 Ibid, Appendix G.

41 See 'Peatland carbon stocks and burn history: Blanket bog peat core evidence highlights charcoal impacts on peat physical properties and long-term carbon storage', by A. Heinemeyer et al., 2018. In *GEO*, Volume 5(2). DOI: 10.1002/geo2.63

42 See 'Global response of fire activity to late Quaternary grazer extinctions', 2021, by A.T. Karp, et al. See note ch3, 30.

Chapter 4

1 From *A Naturalist in the Highlands 1767–1771*. See note ch1, 6.

2 From *The Northern Isles: Orkney and Shetland*. See note ch2, 40.

3 In his book *The Drove Roads of Scotland*, p. 33. See note ch1, 7.

4 *Reminiscences of my Life in the Highlands, Volumes 1&2*, by Joseph Mitchell. Reprint in 1971 of the original 1883 edition by David and Charles.

5 *The Finest Road in the World*, by James Miller, gives a detailed overview of the development of the transport networks in the Highlands. See note 58. For a case study of how a remote area of the Highlands became increasingly accessible over the years, see *Escaping Isolation: How Gairloch joined the world*, by Jeremy Fenton, 2020. Available from the Gairloch Museum.

6 During a visit to Strathspey. In Circuit Journeys. See note ch1, 6.

7 See *The Scottish Clearances: A History of the Dispossessed*, by Tom Devine. See note ch2, 36.

8 Quoted in Christopher Dingwall, *The Falls of Bruar, A Garden in the Wild*, 1987.

9 From *A Naturalist in the Highlands*, p. 155. See note ch1, 6.

10 See the chapter 'A Nation of Planters: Introducing the New Trees 1650–1900', by Syd House and Christopher Dingwall. *In People and Woods in Scotland: A History*, edited by T.C. Smout and published in 2003 by Edinburgh University Press.

11 See *The Dam Builders: Power from the Glens* by James Miller for an excellent description of the work involved. Published in 2002 by Birlinn, Edinburgh.

12 The mountain itself is 'Cairn Gorm' but the general area is 'the Cairngorm Mountains' or 'the Cairngorms', or just 'Cairngorm'.

13 From a paper by O.H. Mackenzie given to the Inverness Field Club. See note ch2, 13.

Chapter 5

1 The five were Loch Torridon-Loch Broom-Loch Maree in Wester Ross; The Cairngorms; Ben Nevis-Glencoe-Black Mount; Glen Affric-Glen Cannich-Strath Farrar in Inverness-shire; and Loch Lomond-Trossachs. For a history of National Parks in Scotland see *Unfinished Business: A National Parks Strategy for Scotland* published in 2013 by the Scottish Campaign for National Parks and the Association for the Protection of Rural Scotland.

2 See NatureScot's website for further information on National Scenic Areas.

3 For an introduction to how landscapes are assessed see *An Introduction to Landscape*, 2020, by James H.C. Fenton. Published online at https://www.fenton.scot/recent.htm.

4 See NatureScot's website for further information on Wild Land Areas.

5 The Scottish Government's National Planning Framework 4: https://www.gov.scot/publications/national-planning-framework-4/.

6 Designations under the European Commission's Habitats and Species directives.

7 The Unna Principles were laid out in a letter from Percy Unna to the National Trust for Scotland in 1937.

About the author

Dr James H.C. Fenton spent his formative years in Wester Ross and after obtaining a degree in botany from the University of Durham he worked as an ecologist for the British Antarctic Survey studying the moss peat of Antarctica. During his time he gained a PhD from the University of London.

Author and family on the shores of Loch Ness.

Thereafter James taught ecology at a field centre in the English Lake District for five years before returning to Scotland to become one of the first independent consultant ecologists. He carried out ecological surveys for various organisations including the Forestry Commission, the Scottish Wildlife Trust and private landowners. James joined the National Trust for Scotland as their first ecologist in 1991 and remained with the organisation for fourteen years. He carried out ecological surveys of the Trust's landholding, from Unst in the Shetlands to Threave in Galloway. He left in 2005 to join Scottish Natural Heritage, to work on landscape policy in the then National Strategy Unit.

In 2011 he became CEO of Falklands Conservation, the main conservation NGO in the Falkland Islands. Thereafter he returned to Scotland where he lives on the Isle of Seil with his wife Sue and now concentrates on writing. As will be seen from this book, James retains a passion for the traditional Highland landscape.

From 2015–23 he served on the Board of the National Trust for Scotland and is currently the editor of the Scottish Wild Land Group's periodical *Wild Land News*.

www.fenton.scot

Other books by James H.C. Fenton

An Illustrated Book of Peat. The life and death of bogs: A new synthesis, published in 2021.
"This book is essential reading for all students of peatlands." *International Peatland Society*

A Field Guide to Ice, 3rd edition, published in 2023.
"There is a great value to polar travelers in carrying this booklet with them, and it makes for a good little gift to a student or friend traveling to the Arctic and Antarctic regions." *Arctic, Antarctic, & Alpine Research*

Acknowledgements

This book has been written after many years of observation and cogitation, so I would like to thank everyone who has put up with my discussions and arguments over that time. I would particularly like to thank my wife, Sue, and my brother, Jeremy, who took time to comment on the text, and to Rose Wands who brought her proofreading skills to bear.